W9-ANO-871

At Sylvan, we believe that a lifelong love of learning begins at an early age, and we are glad you have chosen our resources to help your children experience both the joy of mathematics and the joy of reading as they build these critical skills. We know that the time you spend with your children reinforcing the lessons learned in school will contribute to their love of learning.

A love of reading will translate into academic achievement. A successful reader is ready for the world around him, ready to do research, ready to experience the world of literature, and prepared to make the connections necessary to achieve in school and in life. Similarly, success in math requires more than just memorizing basic facts and algorithms; it also requires children to make sense of size, shape, and numbers as they appear in the world. Children who can connect their understanding of math to the world around them will be ready for the challenges of mathematics as they advance to more complex topics.

We use a research-based, step-by-step process in teaching both reading and math at Sylvan that includes thought-provoking reading selections, math problems, and activities. As students increase their success as learners, they become more confident. With increasing confidence, students build even more success. The design of the Sylvan workbooks will help you to help your children build the skills and confidence that will contribute to success in school.

Included with your purchase of this workbook is a coupon for a discount at a participating Sylvan center. We hope you will use this coupon to further your child's academic journey. Let us partner with you to support the development of a confident, well prepared, independent learner.

The Sylvan Team

Sylvan Learning Center.
Unleash your child's potential here.

No matter how big or small the academic challenge, every child has the ability to learn. But sometimes children need help making it happen. Sylvan believes every child has the potential to do great things. And, we know better than anyone else how to tap into that academic potential so that a child's future really is full of possibilities. Sylvan Learning Center is the place where your child can build and master the learning skills needed to succeed and unlock the potential you know is there.

The proven, personalized approach of our in-center programs deliver unparalleled results that other supplemental education services simply can't match. Your child's achievements will be seen not only in test scores and report cards but outside the classroom as well. And when he starts achieving his full potential, everyone will know it. You will see a new level of confidence come through in everything he does and every interaction he has.

How can Sylvan's personalized in-center approach help your child unleash his potential?

• Starting with our exclusive Sylvan Skills Assessment®, we pinpoint your child's exact academic needs.

• Then we develop a customized learning plan designed to achieve your child's academic goals.

• Through our method of skill mastery, your child will not only learn and master every skill in his personalized plan, he will be truly motivated and inspired to achieve his full potential.

To get started, included with this Sylvan product purchase is $10 off our exclusive Sylvan Skills Assessment®. Simply use this coupon and contact your local Sylvan Learning Center to set up your appointment.

And to learn more about Sylvan and our innovative in-center programs, call 1-800-EDUCATE or visit www.SylvanLearning.com. *With over 1,000 locations in North America, there is a Sylvan Learning Center near you!*

Kindergarten
Reading & Math
Workout

Copyright © 2014 by Sylvan Learning, Inc.

All rights reserved.

Published in the United States by Random House LLC, New York, and in Canada by Random House of Canada Limited, Toronto.

A Penguin Random House Company.

www.tutoring.sylvanlearning.com

Created by Smarterville Productions LLC
Producer: TJ Trochlil McGreevy
Producer & Editorial Direction: The Linguistic Edge
Writers: Amy Kraft and Erin Lassiter
Cover and Interior Illustrations: Shawn Finley and Duendes del Sur
Layout and Art Direction: SunDried Penguin
Art Manager: Adina Ficano
Director of Product Development: Russell Ginns

First Edition

ISBN: 978-1-101-88187-3

Library of Congress Cataloging-in-Publication Data available upon request.

This book is available at special discounts for bulk purchases for sales promotions or premiums. For more information, write to Special Markets/Premium Sales, 1745 Broadway, MD 6-2, New York, New York 10019 or e-mail specialmarkets@randomhouse.com.

PRINTED IN CHINA

10 9 8 7 6 5 4 3 2 1

Kindergarten
Reading Readiness

Contents

Letters and Sounds

1. Alphabet Zone ... 2
2. Consonant Sounds ... 6
3. Beginning Sounds ... 28
4. Ending Sounds ... 32
   Review ... 36
5. Short Vowels ... 40
6. Let's Rhyme ... 50

Words, Words, Words

7. Words to Know ... 56
8. More Words to Know ... 60
   Review ... 64
9. Up and Down ... 68
10. Words to Know ... 70
11. Colors ... 74
12. Big and Little ... 78
13. More Words to Know ... 80
14. More Colors ... 84
15. More Words to Know ... 88
    Review ... 92

Reading Comprehension

16. Story Characters ... 96
17. Story Setting ... 100
18. Story Sequence ... 104
19. Story Problem and Solution ... 108
20. Storytelling ... 112
    Review ... 116
    Answers ... 118

Alphabet Letter Search

The alphabet letters are playing hide and seek. CIRCLE each letter when you find it in the picture.

(A) B C D E F G H I J K L M N O P Q R S T U V W X Y Z

Alphabet Maze

FOLLOW the path marked with **lowercase** letters to help the bunny go home.

Complete the Alphabet

FILL IN the chart with the missing letters.

Mm   Ww   Ss   Bb   Ff

Aa Bb Cc Dd Ee

Ff Gg Hh Ii Jj Kk

Ll Mm Nn Oo Pp

Qq Rr Ss Tt Uu

Vv Ww Xx Yy Zz

Match the Letters

DRAW a line to connect the uppercase and lowercase letters that go together.

Consonant Sounds

What's My Sound?

CIRCLE the pictures with the **m** sound.
COLOR the pictures for fun.

Mm

morning sun

my cat

S s

What's My Sound?

DRAW lines from the "Ss" to pictures with the **s** sound. COLOR the pictures for fun.

swine

sapper duck

Hide and Seek

LOOK at the farm. CIRCLE things that start with the f sound.

Ff

L l

2

What's My Sound?

CIRCLE the pictures with the **l** sound.
COLOR the pictures for fun.

Rr

What's My Sound?

DRAW lines from the "Rr" to pictures with the **r** sound.
COLOR the pictures for fun.

T t

Draw It

LOOK at the train. DRAW your own pictures with the **t** sound on the blank train cars.

Hide and Seek

Look at the park. CIRCLE the things and activities in the park that start with the **p** sound.

Pp

Nn

What's My Sound?

DRAW lines from the "Nn" to pictures that start with the **n** sound. COLOR the pictures for fun.

Bb

Draw It

LOOK at the big bag. DRAW your own pictures
with the **b** sound inside the big bag.

Cc

What's My Sound?

DRAW lines from the "Cc" to pictures with the **c** sound. COLOR the pictures for fun.

Hide and Seek

LOOK at the house. CIRCLE the things and activities
in the house that start with the **h** sound.

Gg

What's My Sound?

CIRCLE the pictures with the **g** sound.
COLOR the pictures for fun.

What's My Sound?

DRAW lines from the "Ww" to pictures that start with the **w** sound. COLOR the pictures for fun.

V v

What's My Sound?

CIRCLE the pictures that start with the v sound.
COLOR the pictures for fun.

What's My Sound?

CIRCLE the pictures that start with the **d** sound.
COLOR the pictures for fun.

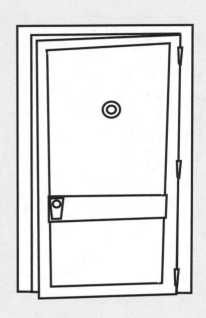

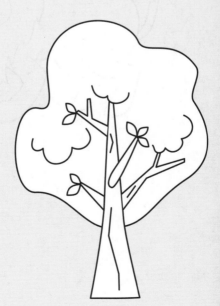

J j

What's My Sound?

DRAW lines from the "Jj" to pictures with the j sound. COLOR the pictures for fun.

J j

Kk

What's My Sound?

DRAW lines from the "Kk" to pictures that start with the k sound.
COLOR the pictures for fun.

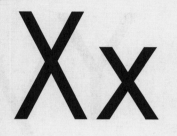

Draw It

LOOK at the box. DRAW your own pictures with the **x** sound inside the box.

NOTE: Words that contain the sound but not the letter, such as **socks**, are okay.

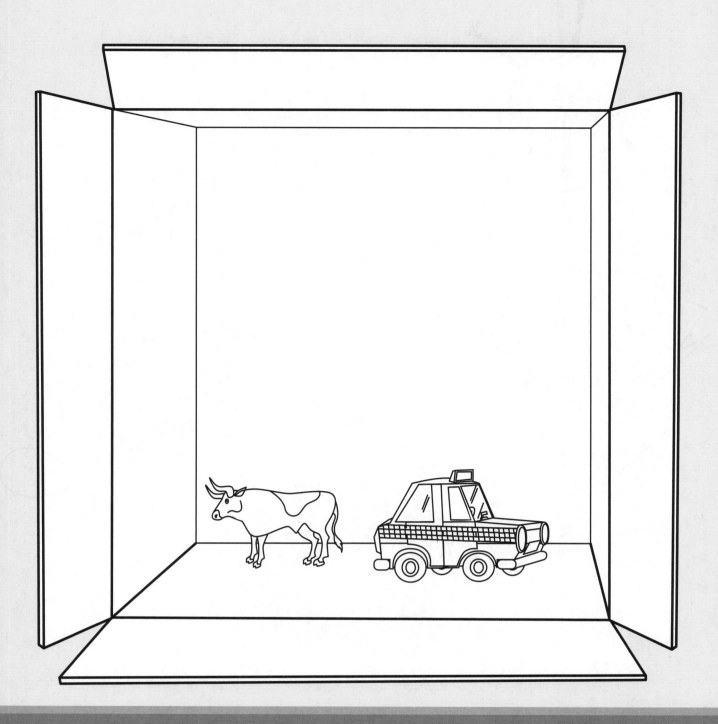

What's My Sound?

CIRCLE the pictures that start with the y sound.
COLOR the pictures for fun.

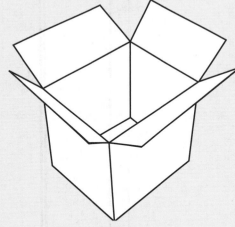

Zz

What's My Sound?

DRAW lines from the "Zz" to pictures that start with the **z** sound.
COLOR the pictures for fun.

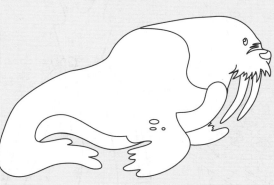

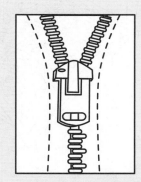

Zz

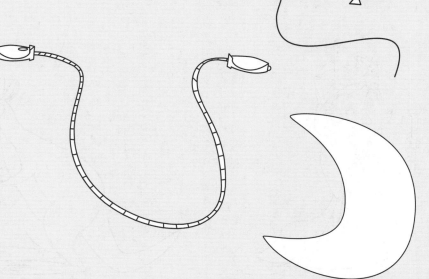

What's My Sound?

DRAW lines from the "qu" to pictures with the **qu** sound.
COLOR the pictures for fun.

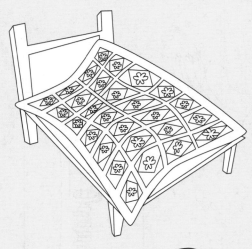

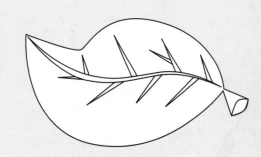

ck

What's My Sound?

DRAW lines from the "ck" to pictures with the **ck** sound. COLOR the pictures for fun.

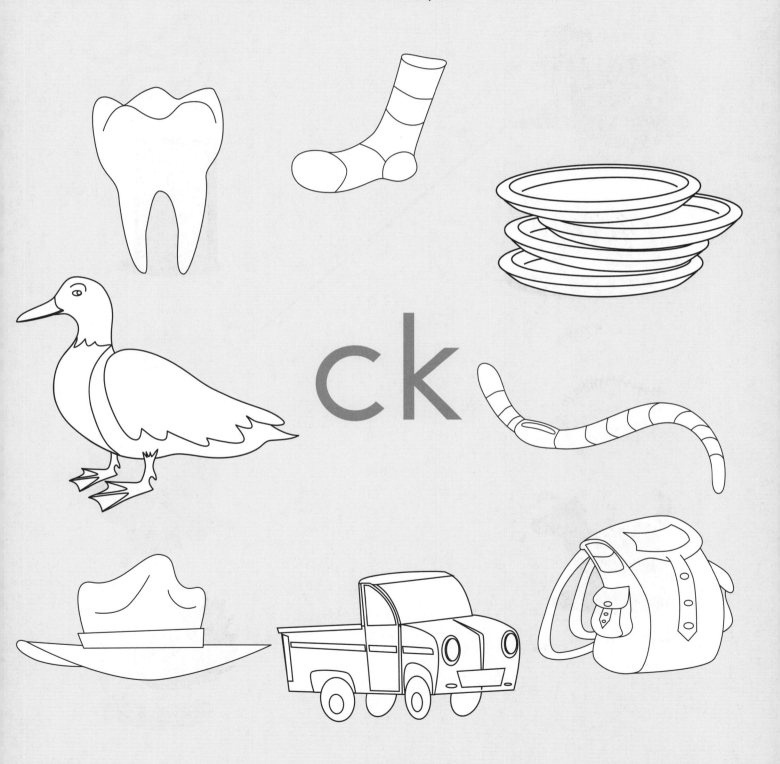

ck

Match Up

LOOK at the pictures. DRAW a line between the pictures that **begin** with the same sound.

Let's do some more!

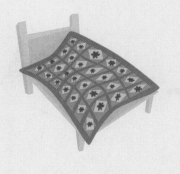

Circle It

LOOK at the letter. CIRCLE the picture in the row that **begins** with the letter sound.

Hh

Nn

Rr

Ww

Starting Line

LOOK at the picture. WRITE the letter that makes the sound at the **beginning** of the word.

Match Up

LOOK at the pictures. DRAW a line between the pictures that **end** with the same sound.

Let's do some more!

Circle It

LOOK at the letter. CIRCLE the picture in the row that **ends** with the letter sound.

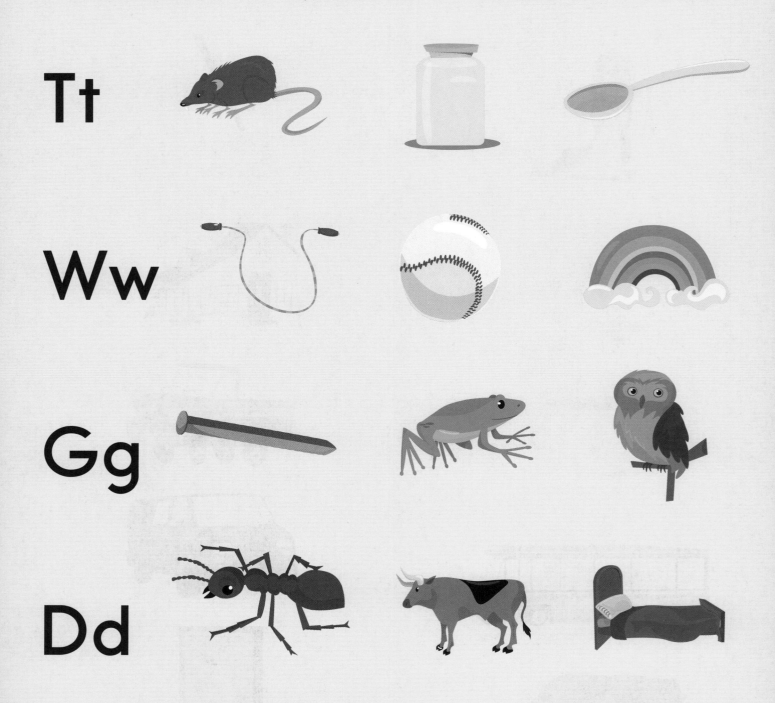

Finish Line

LOOK at the picture. WRITE the letter that makes the sound at the **end** of the word.

_____

- -

_____

1   2   3

_____

- -

_____

4   5   6

Match Up

DRAW a line between each letter and the picture with the same beginning sound.

M

F

L

R

B

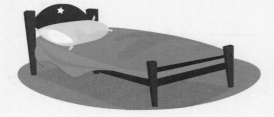

Let's do some more!

N

Z

Y

D

P

Starting Line

WRITE the letter or letters that make the **beginning** sound for each set of pictures.

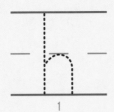

1

2

3

4

5

Finish Line

WRITE the letter that makes the **ending** sound for each set of pictures.

_ _ _
1

_ _ _
2

_ _ _
3

_ _ _
4

_ _ _
5

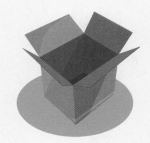

Short Vowels

What's My Sound?

DRAW lines from the "a" to pictures with the short **a** sound.
COLOR the pictures for fun.

What Am I?

MATCH the pictures to the words.

hat

pan

rat

bag

cat

What's My Sound?

DRAW lines from the "e" to pictures with the short **e** sound.
COLOR the pictures for fun.

What Am I?

MATCH the pictures to the words.

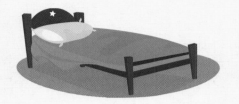

web

hen

ten

net

bed

What's My Sound?

DRAW lines from the "i" to pictures with the short i sound.
COLOR the pictures for fun.

i

What Am I?

MATCH the pictures to the words.

kick

bib

pig

sit

kid

What's My Sound?

DRAW lines from the "o" to pictures with the short **o** sound.
COLOR the pictures for fun.

What Am I?

MATCH the pictures to the words.

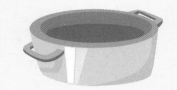

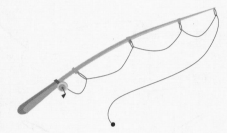

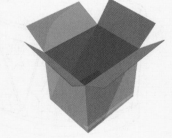

rod

pot

top

mop

box

What's My Sound?

DRAW lines from the "u" to pictures with the short **u** sound.
COLOR the pictures for fun.

U

u

What Am I?

MATCH the pictures to the words.

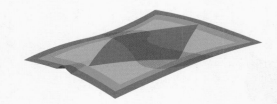

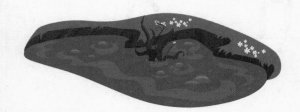

cup

tub

mud

bug

rug

Time to Rhyme

FILL IN the missing letter to make a rhyme to match the picture.

1
f   t   c   t

2
b   g   h   g

Match Up

MATCH the pictures that sound alike.

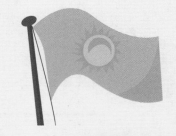

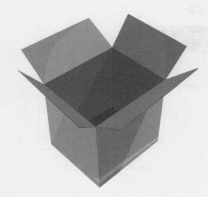

Time to Rhyme

FILL IN the missing letter to make a rhyme to match the picture.

1 _____

m   n   r   n

2 _____

f   n   r   n

Match Up

MATCH the pictures that sound alike.

Time to Rhyme

FILL IN the missing letter to make a rhyme that matches the picture.

1

b g d g

2

p p c p

Match Up

MATCH the pictures that sound alike.

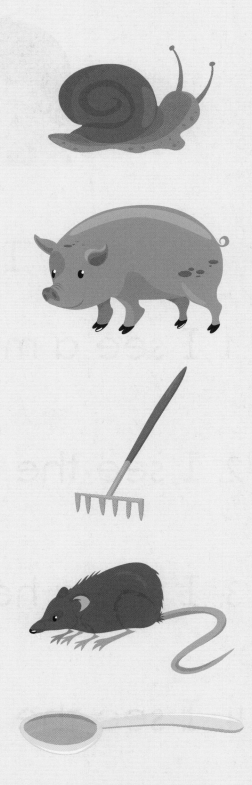

Time to Read

READ each sentence out loud. MATCH the sentences to the pictures.

I see the hat.

1. I see a man.

2. I see the rat.

3. I see a hen.

4. I see the bed.

Make a Book

DRAW a picture to match each sentence.

My Very Own Book
What Do I See?
Pictures by

_____

2

I see a cat.

4

I see a pan.

6

I see a jet.

8

I see a ham.

10

I see a bag.

Turn the page to finish your book.

Words to Know

Finish Your Book

CUT on the dotted lines. ASK a parent to staple the pages together. READ your book out loud. ✂

3

I see the hat.

1

I see the map.

7

I see the van.

5

I see the net.

11

I see the jam.

9

I see a bat.

Find the Missing Word

LOOK at each sentence. LOOK at the words in the word box. WRITE the correct word in each blank. CROSS OUT the words as you use them.

I	a	~~see~~	jet

1. I __see__ the rat.

2. _____ see a man.

3. I see a _____.

4. I see _____ bed.

Time to Read

READ each sentence out loud. MATCH the sentences to the pictures.

1. I see a man and a cat.

2. The pig is wet.

3. I see a fox in a hat.

4. The rat is in the box.

Make a Book

DRAW a picture to match each sentence.

My Very Own Book
What Do I See?
Pictures by

_____

2

I see a man in a jet.

4

The ham is in the pan.

6

The cat is in the bed.

8

It is a big top.

10

It is a red dot.

Turn the page to finish your book.

Finish Your Book

CUT on the dotted lines. ASK a parent to staple the pages together. READ your book out loud. ✂

3

I see a pig in a pen.

1

I see a kid and a pet.

7

The dog is in the van.

5

The rat is in the log.

11

It is a wet mop.

9

It is a hot pot.

Find the Missing Word

LOOK at each sentence. LOOK at the words in the word box. WRITE the correct word in each blank. CROSS OUT the words as you use them.

 It in is and

1. I see a cat _____and_____ a dog.

2. The fox _____is_____ red.

3. _____it_____ is a big net.

4. The fan is _____in_____ the den.

What's My Sound?

LOOK at the vowel. CIRCLE the picture with the same sound.

What's My Sound?

WRITE a letter to match the **middle** sound for each picture.

m a p

b e d
2

w e b
3

t u b
4

k i ck
5

s o ck
6

Match Up

READ each sentence out loud. MATCH the sentences to the pictures.

1. I see a wet dog in a tub.

2. I see a hen and a duck.

3. The red bug is in a net.

4. The pig is in the mud.

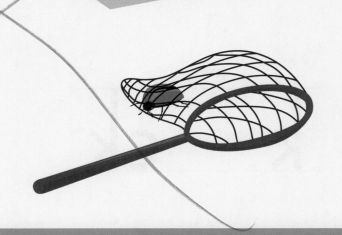

Find the Missing Word

LOOK at each sentence. LOOK at the words in the word box. WRITE the correct word in each blank.

hot	It	and	The

1. _____the_____ box is big and red.

2. I see a pan ____and____ a can.

3. The sun is big and ____hot____.

4. _____It_____ is ham in a can.

Up and Down

Circle It

LOOK at the word. CIRCLE the picture that matches the word.

up   **down**

1. up

2. up

3. down

4. down

Which Way?

WRITE the word "up" or "down" to match the picture.

1. The jet is _____up_____.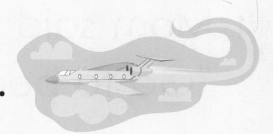

2. The man is _____up_____.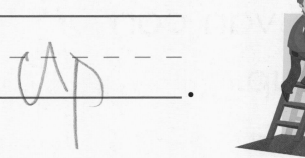

3. The jet is _____down_____.

4. The man is _____down_____.

Time to Read

MATCH the sentences to the pictures. READ each sentence out loud.

1. Mom said,
   "Go to bed."

2. The van can
   go up.

3. I see you in
   the bus.

4. Liz said "sit"
   to the dog.

Words to Know

10

Make a Book

DRAW a picture to match each sentence.

My Very Own Book

The Story of Nan and Pat

Pictures by

_____

2

Pat had a rat.

4

Pat saw Nan.

6

Nan said, "Yes, you can pet the dog."

8

Pat said, "Yes, you can pet the rat."

10

Nan pet the rat.

Turn the page to finish your book.

Finish Your Book

CUT on the dotted lines. ASK a parent to staple the pages together. READ your book out loud. ✂

3

Nan saw Pat.

1

Nan had a dog.

7

Nan said, "Can I pet the rat?"

5

Pat said, "Can I pet the dog?"

11

The dog and the rat had a nap.

9

Pat pet the dog.

Find the Missing Word

LOOK at each sentence. LOOK at the words in the word box. WRITE the correct word in each blank. CROSS OUT the words as you use them.

said	go	to	down

1. You _____ up in the jet.

2. I sit _____ in the jet.

3. You _____, "It is fun."

4. The dog ran _____ the man.

Colors

Time to Read

LOOK at the color word. CIRCLE the picture that matches the color.

red	green	blue	yellow

1. red

2. green

3. blue

4. yellow

Make a Book

DRAW a picture to match each sentence.

My Very Own Book

Red, Green, Blue, and Yellow

Pictures by

_____

2

The sack is blue.

4

The sun is yellow.

6

The bed is blue.

8

The bug is yellow.

10

The bus is yellow.

Turn the page to finish your book.

Finish Your Book

CUT on the dotted lines. ASK a parent to staple the pages together. READ your book out loud.

3

The cup is red.

1

The box is green.

7

The fox is red.

5

The sock is green.

11

The hat is red.

9

The jet is blue.

Draw It

READ each color word out loud. DRAW three things the same color inside each square.

yellow	red
blue	**green**

Circle It

LOOK at the word. CIRCLE the picture that matches the word.

big	little

1. big

2. little

3. big

4. little

Blank Out

WRITE the word "big" or "little" to match the picture.

1. The van is _____.

2. The egg is _____.

3. The top is _____.

4. The bed is _____.

Match Up

READ each sentence out loud. MATCH the sentences to the pictures.

1. I have a green box.

2. I have a yellow box for you.

3. The rat is on the big rug.

4. We have a blue sack.

Make a Book

DRAW a picture to match each sentence.

My Very Own Book

A Dog, a Cat, and Hats

Pictures by

_____

2

We have a little cat.

4

The cat is on the rug.

6

We have a red hat for the cat.

8

We put the red hat on the cat.

10

We hug the cat.

Turn the page to finish your book.

Finish Your Book

CUT on the dotted lines. ASK a parent to staple the pages together. READ your book out loud. ✂

3

The dog is on the rug.

1

We have a big dog.

7

We put the blue hat on the dog.

5

We have a blue hat for the dog.

11

We have a dog and a cat in hats.

9

We hug the dog.

Find the Missing Word

LOOK at each sentence. LOOK at the words in the word box. WRITE the correct word in each blank. CROSS OUT the words as you use them.

for	have	on	We

1. We _____ a big van.

2. The mud is _____ the rug.

3. I have a job _____ you.

4. _____ see the yellow bus.

Match Up

LOOK at the color word. CIRCLE the picture in the row that matches the color.

orange   **purple**   **black**   **brown**

1. orange

2. purple

3. black

4. brown

Make a Book

DRAW a picture to match each sentence.

My Very Own Book

Colors

Pictures by

_____

2

The bat is black.

4

The log is brown.

6

The rock is brown.

8

The mud is brown.

10

The pan is black.

Turn the page to finish your book.

Finish Your Book

CUT on the dotted lines. ASK a parent to staple the pages together. READ your book out loud. ✂

3

The rug is purple.

1

The cat is orange.

7

The jam is purple.

5

The van is orange.

11

The hat is purple.

9

The yam is orange.

Draw It

READ each color word out loud. DRAW three things the same color inside each square.

orange	purple
black	**brown**

Match Up

READ each sentence out loud. MATCH the sentences to the pictures.

1. We look at the map.

2. She is not on the bus.

3. He is not sad.

4. We look for a bug.

Draw the Story

READ the story out loud.

The Bus

I get on the bus. I see Sam. He is on the bus. I see Gus. He is on the bus. I see Pam. She is on the bus. We sit on the bus.

DRAW a picture to match the story.

Find the Missing Word

LOOK at each sentence. LOOK at the words in the word box. WRITE the correct word in each blank. CROSS OUT the words as you use them.

He   not   is   look

1. I _____ in the den for

the dog.

2. _____ is a big man.

3. The duck is _____ purple.

4. She _____ a brown hen.

Draw the Story

READ the story out loud.

The Pig

I have a pet pig. He is a little pig. He is a black pig. He is not a mad pig. He is not a sad pig. He is a fun pig.

DRAW a picture to match the story.

What Color Am I?

MATCH the color words to the pictures.

purple

yellow

orange

black

blue

Word Puzzles

CUT OUT the words. USE the words to create your own sentences.

The	the	the	I
and	see	have	go
You	you	a	a
She	she	is	can
He	he	to	for
little	on	in	big
duck	dog	cat	pig
bed	hat	rug	bug
bus	jet	yellow	brown
black	green	red	blue

Words I Know

LOOK at the words. READ each word out loud.

I	a	you	said
the	see	have	on
and	is	we	for
in	it	not	look
down	up	he	she
go	to	big	little

Story Characters

Who Is It?

The people and the animals in a story are the **characters**.

Animals

People

CIRCLE the pictures that can be characters in a story.

Who Is It?

READ the story out loud.

The Mud

The pig is in the mud. The dog is in the mud. The rat is in the mud. The hen is in the mud. The mud is brown. The mud is wet. It is fun.

CIRCLE the characters in the story.

Who Is It?

READ the story out loud.

The Mat

The duck ran to the man. The cat ran to the man. The duck sat on the mat. The cat sat on the mat. The man fed the duck and the cat on the mat.

CIRCLE the characters in the story.

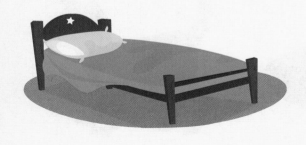

Who Is It?

READ the story out loud.

The Rat

A kid sat on a big rock. A dog sat on the rock. A cat sat on the rock. The kid said, "I see a rat." The cat ran. The dog ran. The kid ran.

DRAW the characters in the story.

Story Setting

Where Is It?

The place and time in a story create the **setting**.

Place

Time

CIRCLE the pictures that can be the setting for a story.

Where Is It?

READ the story out loud.

The Cat

I look for the cat. I look on the bed. The cat is not on the bed. I look on the rug. The cat is not on the rug. I look in a big box. I see the cat. It is in the big box.

CIRCLE the setting for the story.

Where Is It?

READ the story out loud.

The Run

He can run. She can run. I can run. You can run. We run to the rock. We run to the log. It is hot. We run in the sun.

CIRCLE the setting for the story.

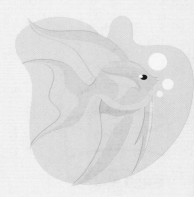

Where Is It?

READ the story out loud.

The Van

Dad is in the van. I get in the van. You get in the van. We look at the map. We go up. We go down. We go and go in the van.

DRAW the setting for the story.

Story Sequence

What's the Order?

READ the story out loud.

> ### Jam and Ham
>
> I have a pot. I put ham in the pot. I put jam in the pot. I mix the ham and jam. Yum!

WRITE 1, 2, and 3 to show the beginning, middle, and end of the story.

_____   _____   _____

What's the Order?

A story has a beginning, a middle, and an end.

LOOK at the pictures. WRITE 1, 2, and 3 to show the correct order.

_____

_____

_____

_____

_____

_____

What's the Order?

READ the story out loud. DRAW the beginning, middle, and end of the story.

The Dog

I put the dog in the tub. I rub the dog. I put the dog in the sun.

1	2	3

What's the Order?

READ the story out loud. DRAW the beginning, middle, and end of the story.

The Cat Nap

I sit on the bed. I pat the cat.

I take a nap with the cat.

1	2	3

Story Problem and Solution

What's the Solution?

Most stories have a problem and a solution.

For example:

| Problem | Solution |

LOOK at the problem. DRAW the solution.

| Problem | Solution |

What's the Solution?

LOOK at the problem.

Problem

CIRCLE the correct solution to the problem.

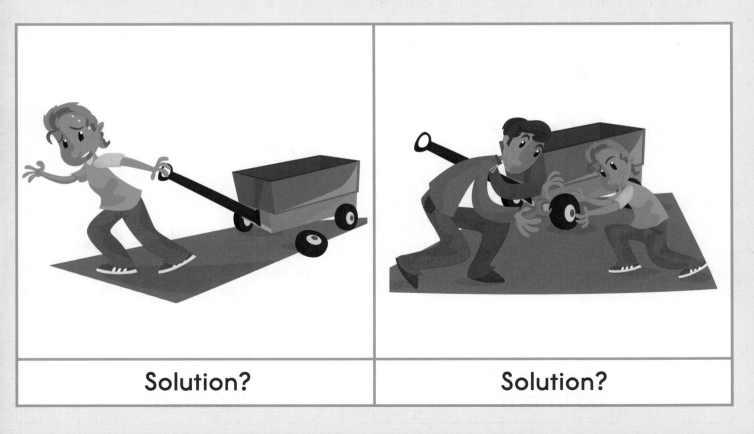

Solution?   Solution?

Story Problem and Solution

What's the Solution?

LOOK at the problem.

Problem

CIRCLE the correct solution to the problem.

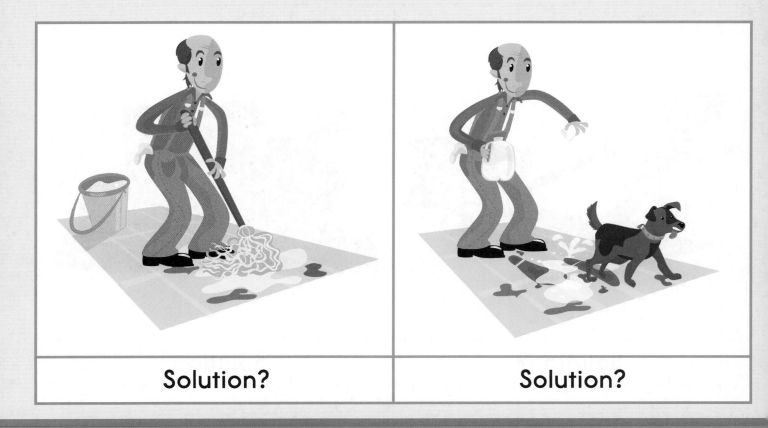

Solution?   Solution?

What's the Solution?

READ the story out loud.

> ### Ben
>
> Ben hid. I look in the den. Ben is not in the den. I look in the tub. I see Ben. He is in the tub.

DRAW the problem in the story. DRAW the solution in the story.

Problem	**Solution**

Draw the Story

READ the story out loud. DRAW a picture to answer each question about the story.

Meg

Meg is sick. She is in bed. She is sad. I have a dog. I go to see Meg. I put the dog on the bed. Meg can pet the dog on his back. The dog can lick Meg on the neck. Meg is sick. But she is not sad.

Who is it?

Where is it?

What is the problem?

What is the solution?

Storytelling

Draw the Story

READ the story out loud. DRAW what happens in the story in the correct order.

The Bug

A bug is on the pig. The pig is mad. I go to get a net. I get the bug in the net. I see a rock. I put the bug on the rock.

1	**2**

3

4

5

6

Who, Where, and What?

CIRCLE the picture that can be a character in a story.

 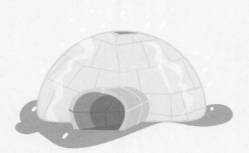 

CIRCLE the picture that can be the setting for a story.

CIRCLE the picture that can be a problem in a story.

What's the Story?

WRITE 1, 2, and 3, to show the beginning, middle, and end of the story.

CIRCLE the square that shows and tells the **problem** in the story.

I fan the dog in the sun.

_____

The dog is hot in the sun.

_____

I go get a fan.

_____

Answers

Page 2

Page 3

Page 4
1. Bb 2. Ff 3. Mm 4. Ss 5. Ww

Page 5

Page 6
mouse, moon, mitten, map, monkey

Page 7
sun, snail, stop, spoon, star

Page 8
fish, fence, frog, flies, flowers, farmer, face, fruit, flag, fan

Page 9
leaf, lightbulb, ladybug, ladder

Page 10
rainbow, rocket, robot, ring, rake

Page 11
Suggestions: tree, top, teeth, toothbrush, turkey, TV, table, toys, teacher, tea, tie, telephone

Page 12
police, play, path, picnic, pizza, piece of pizza, pie, purse, parrot, paint, painter, painting, person, puppy, post, picnic basket

Page 13
nose, net, nail, nine, nest

Page 14
Suggestions: bat, bug, boy, bread, butter, bottle, bone, bowl, button, bow, balloon, banana, belt

Page 15
car, carrot, corn, cake, cow

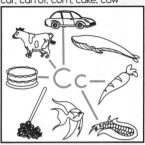

Page 16
ham, horse, hat, hang, hanger, hammer, heart, hair, hat stand, hands

Page 17
glasses, girl, goat, grapes

Page 18
whale, wagon, walrus, worm, window

Page 19
volcano, violin, van, vegetables

Page 20
door, dress, dishes, doll

Page 21
juice box, jar, jellyfish, jump rope

Answers

Page 22
kitten, kangaroo, kick, key

Page 23
Suggestions (can contain letter or sound): ox, taxi, fox, box, ax, six, rocks, socks, trucks, ducks, names with the x sound like Max or Rex

Page 24
yarn, yo-yo

Page 25
zebra, zipper, zoo

Page 26
quilt, question mark, queen

Page 27
sock, backpack, truck, duck

Page 28

Page 29

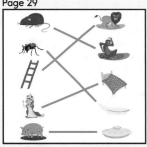

Page 30

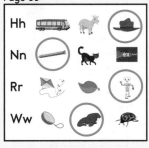

Page 31
1. m, 2. c (or k), 3. b, 4. d, 5. s, 6. l

Page 32

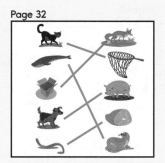

Page 33

Page 34

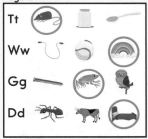

Page 35
1. n, 2. t, 3. l
4. m, 5. s, 6. g

Page 36

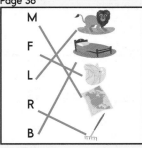

Page 37

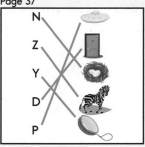

Page 38
1. h, 2. j, 3. v, 4. w, 5. qu

Page 39
1. g, 2. n, 3. s, 4. x, 5. t

Page 40
fan, map, rat, ham, bat

Page 41

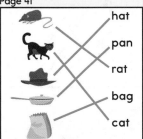

hat
pan
rat
bag
cat

Page 42
nest, net, egg, dress, bed

119

Answers

Page 43
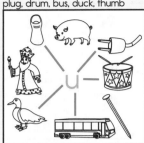
web
hen
ten
net
bed

Page 44
pig, zipper, fish, six, bib
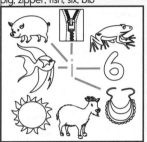

Page 45
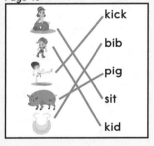
kick
bib
pig
sit
kid

Page 46
dog, lobster, mop, socks, box

Pages 47
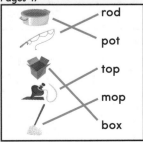
rod
pot
top
mop
box

Page 48
plug, drum, bus, duck, thumb
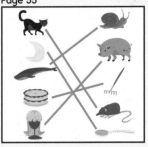

Page 49
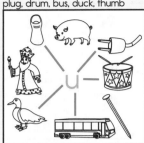
cup
tub
mud
bug
rug

Page 50
1. fat cat
2. bug hug

Page 51
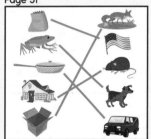

Page 52
1. man ran
2. fun run

Page 53

Page 54
1. big dig
2. pup cup

Page 55

Page 56
1. I see a man.
2. I see the rat.
3. I see a hen.
4. I see the bed.
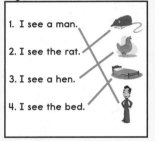

Pages 57–58
Each picture should match the sentence.

Page 59
1. I **see** the rat.
2. **I** see a man.
3. I see a **jet**.
4. I see **a** bed.

Page 60
1. I see a man and a cat.
2. The pig is wet.
3. It is a fox in a hat.
4. The rat is in the box.
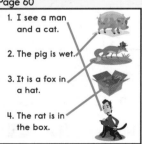

Pages 61–62
Each picture should match the sentence.

Page 63
1. I see a cat **and** a dog.
2. The fox **is** red.
3. **It** is a big net.
4. The fan is **in** the den.

Page 64
a
e
i
o
u

Page 65
1. map, 2. bed, 3. web, 4. tub, 5. kick, 6. sock

Page 66
1. I see a wet dog in a tub.
2. It is a hen and a duck.
3. The red bug is in a net.
4. The pig is in the mud.

Page 67
1. **The** box is big and red.
2. I see a pan **and** a can.
3. The sun is big and **hot**.
4. **It** is ham in a can.

Page 68
1. up
2. up
3. down
4. down
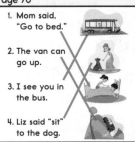

Page 69
1. The jet is **up**.
2. The man is **up**.
3. The jet is **down**.
4. The man is **down**.

Page 70
1. Mom said, "Go to bed."
2. The van can go up.
3. I see you in the bus.
4. Liz said "sit" to the dog.

120

Answers

Pages 71–72
Each picture should match the sentence.

Page 73
1. You **go** up in the jet.
2. I sit **down** in the jet.
3. You **said**, "It is fun."
4. The dog ran **to** the man.

Page 74
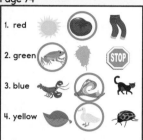
1. red
2. green
3. blue
4. yellow

Pages 75–76
Each picture should match the sentence.

Page 77
Suggestions:
yellow: school bus, sun, duck
red: fire engine, stop sign, apple
blue: whale, water, blueberry
green: tree, leaf, dragon

Page 78
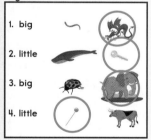
1. big
2. little
3. big
4. little

Page 79
1. The van is **big**.
2. The egg is **little**.
3. The top is **little**.
4. The bed is **big**.

Page 80
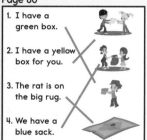
1. I have a green box.
2. I have a yellow box for you.
3. The rat is on the big rug.
4. We have a blue sack.

Pages 81–82
Each picture should match the sentence.

Page 83
1. We **have** a big van.
2. The mud is **on** the rug.
3. I have a job **for** you.
4. **We** see the yellow bus.

Page 84
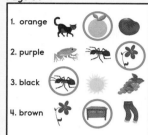
1. orange
2. purple
3. black
4. brown

Pages 85–86
Each picture should match the sentence.

Page 87
Suggestions:
orange: orange, goldfish
purple: flower, plum
black: ant, blackberry, road
brown: paper bag, mud, desk

Page 88

1. We look at the map.
2. She is not on the bus.
3. He is not sad.
4. We look for a bug.

Page 89
The picture should match the story.

Page 90
1. I **look** in the den for the dog.
2. **He** is a big man.
3. The duck is **not** purple.
4. She **is** a brown hen.

Page 91
The picture should match the story.

Page 92
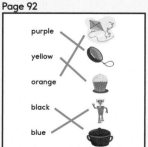
purple
yellow
orange
black
blue

Page 96
queen, cow, doctor, lion

Page 97
pig, dog, rat, hen
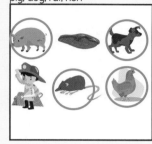

Page 98
man, cat, duck

Page 99
Pictures of a kid, a dog, a cat, and a rat

Page 100
house, barn, night

Page 101

Page 102

Page 103
Picture of a van on a road (on a hill)

Page 104
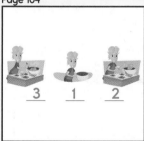
3   1   2

Page 105
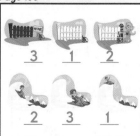
3   1   2
2   3   1

Page 106
Pictures should match the story sequence.

Page 107
Pictures should match the story sequence.

Page 108
Picture should show a solution to the problem.

Answers

Page 109

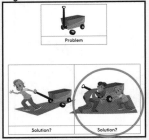

Page 110

Page 111
Pictures should match the story problem and solution.

Pages 112–113
Pictures should match the parts of the story.

Pages 114–115
Pictures should show the story events in order.

Page 116
unicorn, city, kite stuck in tree

Page 117

Kindergarten
Basic Math Success

Contents

Numbers

1 Counting to 5   126

2 Counting to 10   136

3 Zero   148

4 More or Less   150

5 Ordinal Numbers   156

Review   160

Sorting, Classification & Patterns

6 Same & Different   166

7 Picture Patterns   172

8 Number Patterns   178

9 Classifying   184

10 Sorting   190

Review   196

Geometry

11 Recognizing Shapes   202

12 Drawing & Comparing Shapes   210

13 On Location   218

Review   222

Measurement

14 Length   226

15 Weight   230

16 Volume   234

Review   238

Answers   242

Counting to 5

Practice the Number 1

TRACE the number 1.
Start at the green arrow.

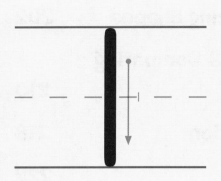

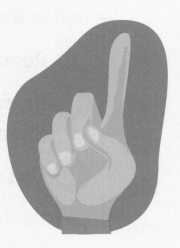

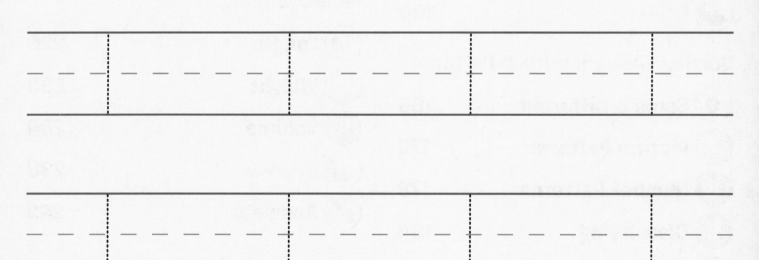

Now WRITE the number 1 next to each picture.

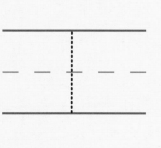

Practice the Number 2

TRACE the number 2.
Start at the green arrow.

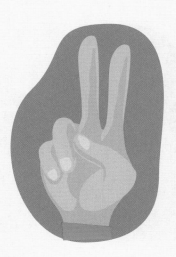

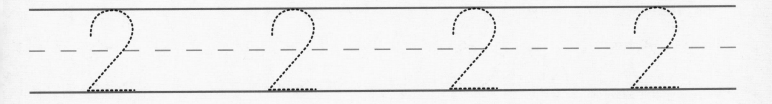

Now WRITE the number **2** next to each picture.

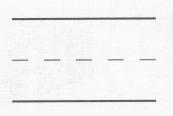

Practice the Number 3

TRACE the number **3**.
Start at the green arrow.

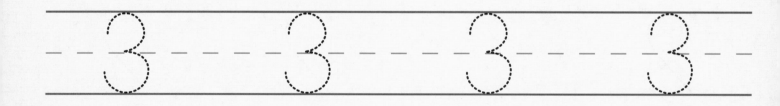

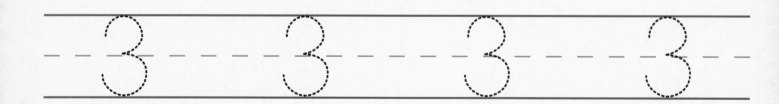

Now WRITE the number **3** next to each picture.

_ _ _ _ _ _ _ _

_ _ _ _ _ _ _ _

Practice the Number 4

TRACE the number 4.
Start at the green arrow.

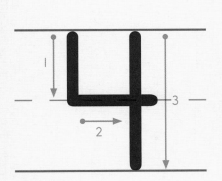

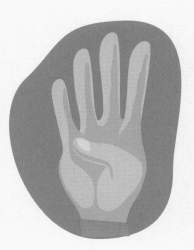

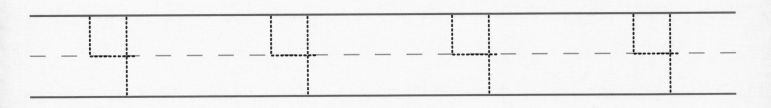

Now WRITE the number 4 next to each picture.

_____

- - - - - - - - - - - - -

_____

_____

- - - - - - - - - - - - -

_____

Practice the Number 5

TRACE the number 5.
Start at the green arrow.

5   5   5   5

5   5   5   5

Now WRITE the number 5 next to each picture.

_____

_____

Color Groups

LOOK at each number. COLOR the correct number of pictures to match the number.

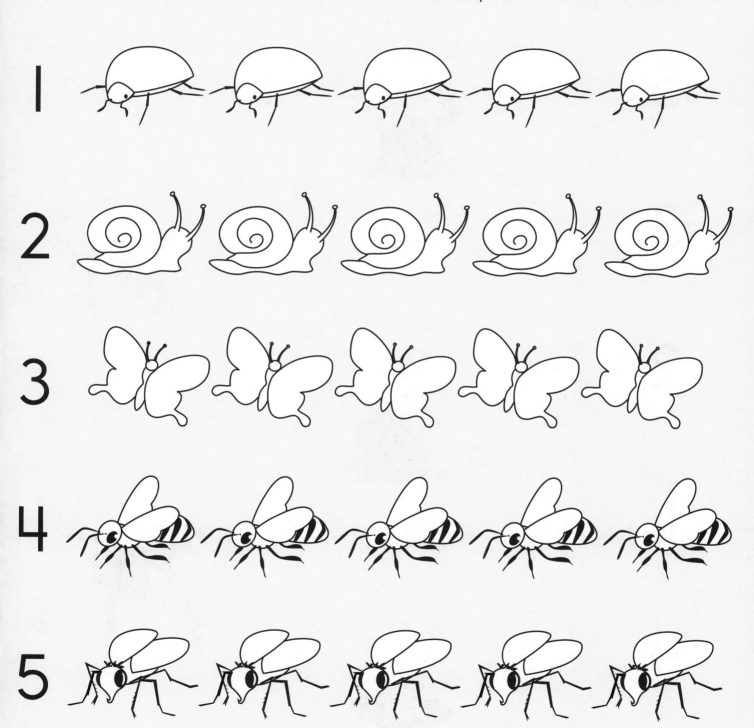

Magic Match Up

DRAW lines to connect the numbers and pictures that go together.

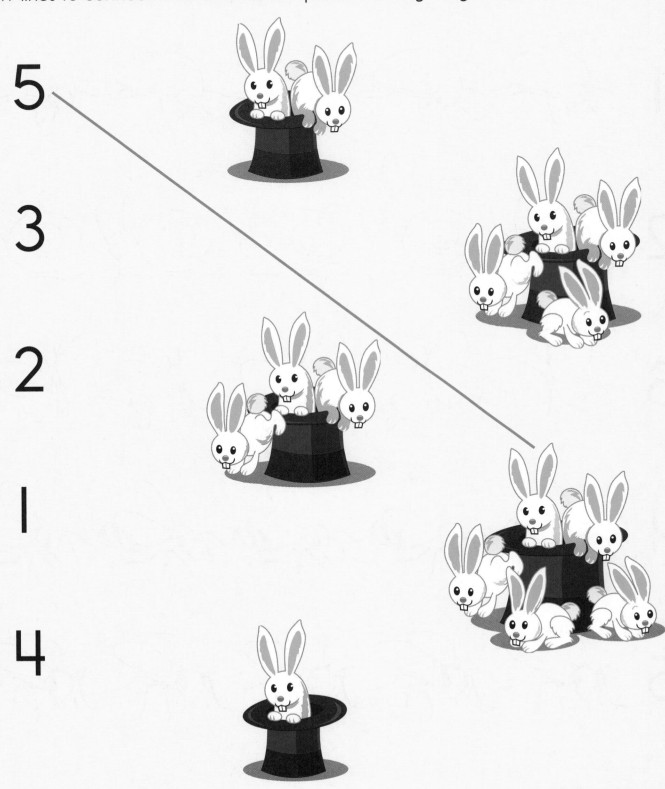

5

3

2

1

4

Loop It

LOOK at each number. CIRCLE the correct number of pictures to match the number.

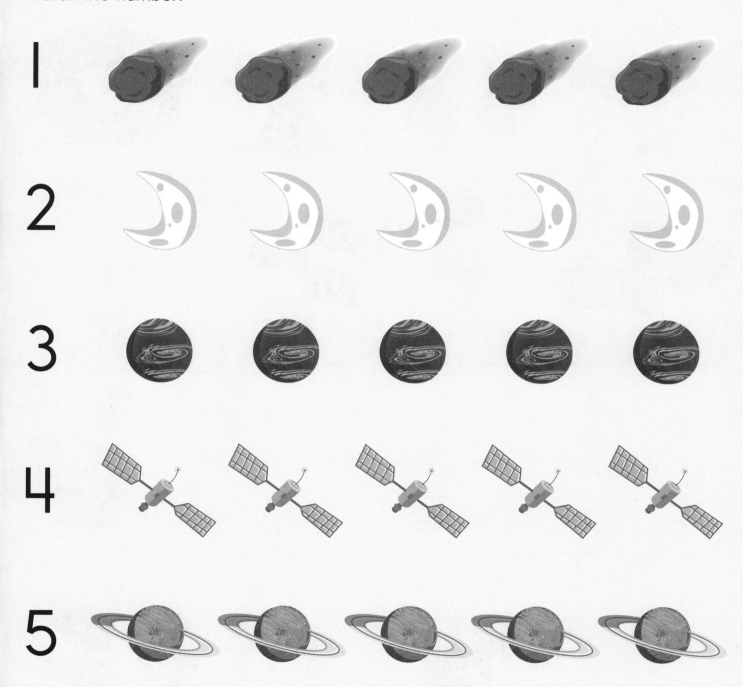

Counting to 5

Odd One Out

CROSS OUT the picture in each row that does **not** go with the others.

134

Hide and Seek

COUNT the number of times each object appears in the picture. Then WRITE the number next to each object.

Practice the Number 6

TRACE the number 6.
Start at the green arrow.

6

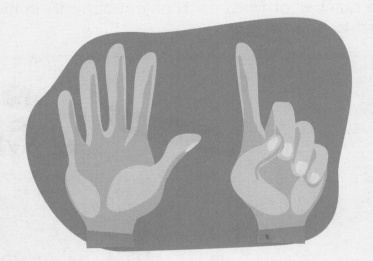

6   6   6   6

6   6   6   6

Now WRITE the number **6** next to each picture.

_____

_____

Practice the Number 7

TRACE the number 7.
Start at the green arrow.

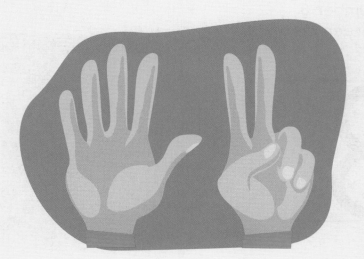

Now WRITE the number **7** next to each picture.

Practice the Number 8

TRACE the number 8.
Start at the green arrow.

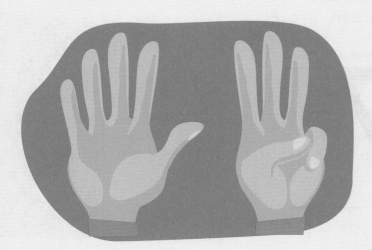

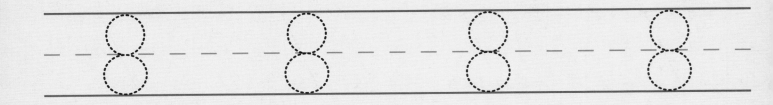

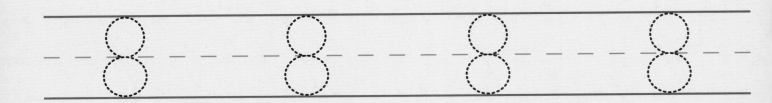

Now WRITE the number 8 next to each picture.

Practice the Number 9

TRACE the number 9.
Start at the green arrow.

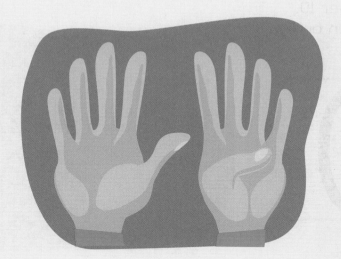

9 9 9 9

9 9 9 9

Now WRITE the number 9 next to each picture.

Practice the Number 10

TRACE the number 10.
Start at the green arrow.

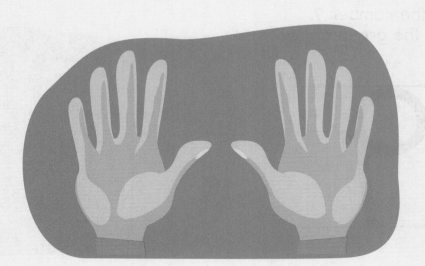

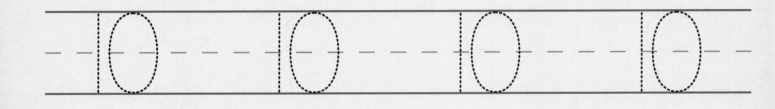

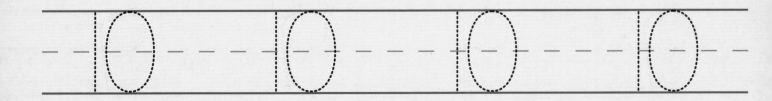

Now WRITE the number 10 next to each picture.

Color Groups

LOOK at each number. COLOR the correct number of pictures to match the number.

6 

7

8

9

10

Fruit Match Up

DRAW lines to connect the numbers and pictures that go together.

7

8

6

10

9

Loop It

LOOK at each number. CIRCLE the correct number of jellybeans to match the number.

6

7

8

9

10

Odd One Out

CROSS OUT the picture in each row that does **not** go with the others.

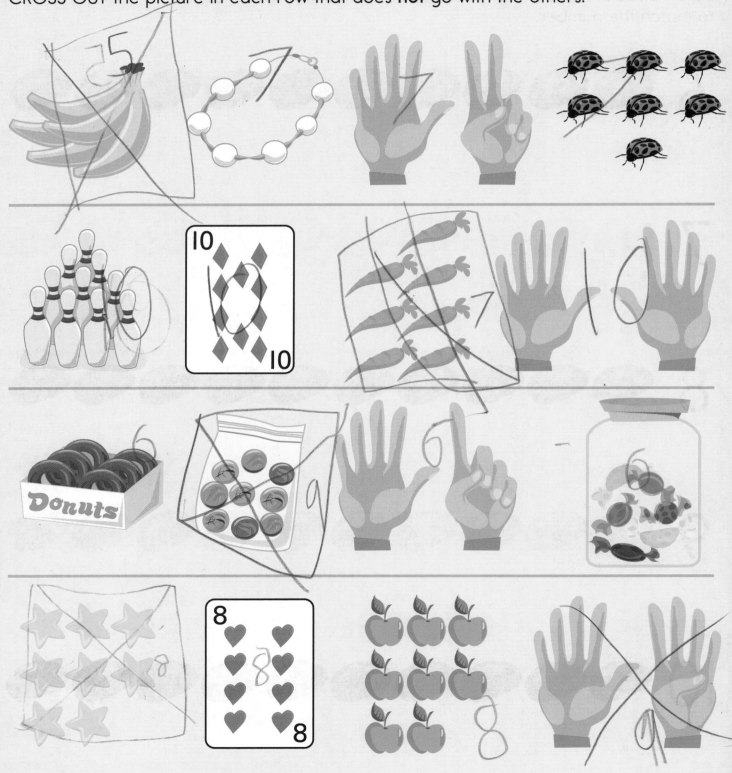

Hide and Seek

COUNT the number of times each object appears in the picture. Then WRITE the number next to each object.

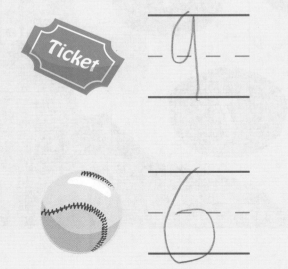

Counting to 10

Pond Crossing

DRAW a line following the numbers 1 through 10 in order, to help the frog jump across the pond.

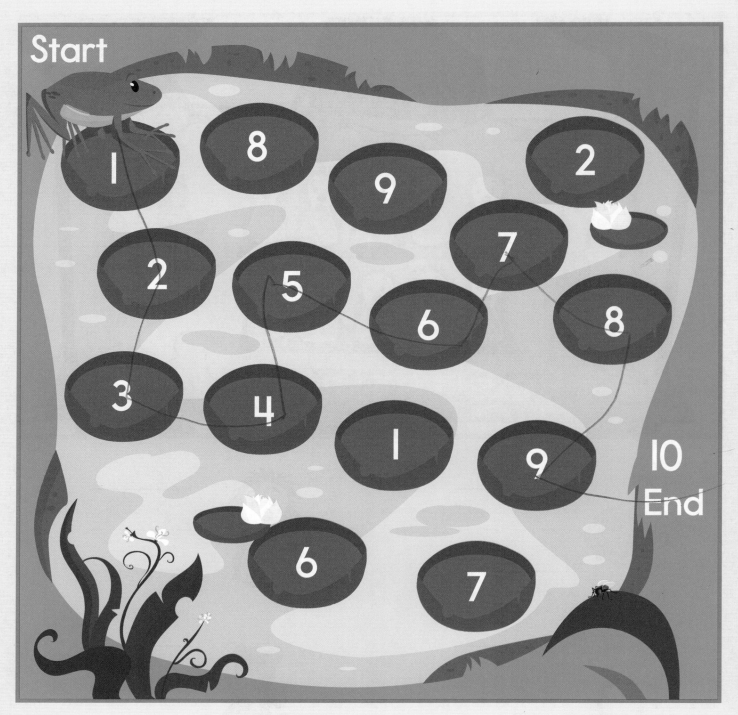

146

Card Tricks

The numbers have disappeared from the cards. WRITE the number for each card.

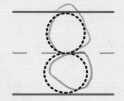

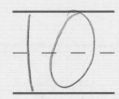

Practice the Number 0

TRACE the number 0.
Start at the green arrow.

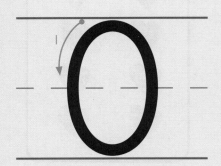

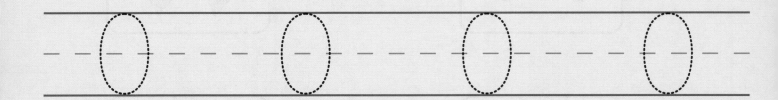

Now WRITE the number **0** next to each picture.

_____

_____

_____

_____

Circle the Same

CIRCLE all of the pictures that show zero.

More or Less

Which One Has More?

CIRCLE the group of fruit that has **more** than the other.

1.

6

3

2.

5

10

3.

2

4

4.

9

8

5.

7

5

6.

4

9

7.

3

7

8.

8

6

Which One Has Less?

CIRCLE the jar on each shelf that has **less** candy than the other.

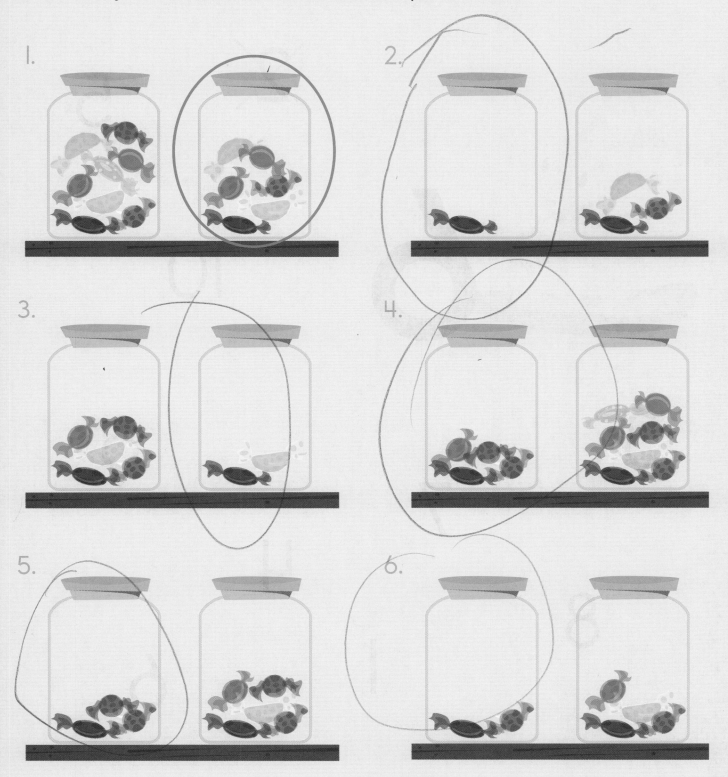

1.

2.

3.

4.

5.

6.

More or Less

Bubble Pop

LOOK at the numbers in the bubbles. CROSS OUT the numbers that are **less** than **6**.

Hide and Seek

COUNT the number of times each fish appears in the picture, and WRITE the number next to each fish. For each pair of fish, CIRCLE the one that has **more** than the other.

7

8

6

5

2

4

More or Less

Card Tricks

CIRCLE the card that has **one more** than the first card.

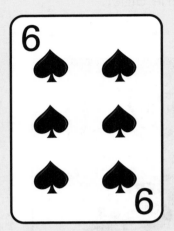

Which One Has Less?

LOOK at each number. CIRCLE the plate that has **one less** than the number.

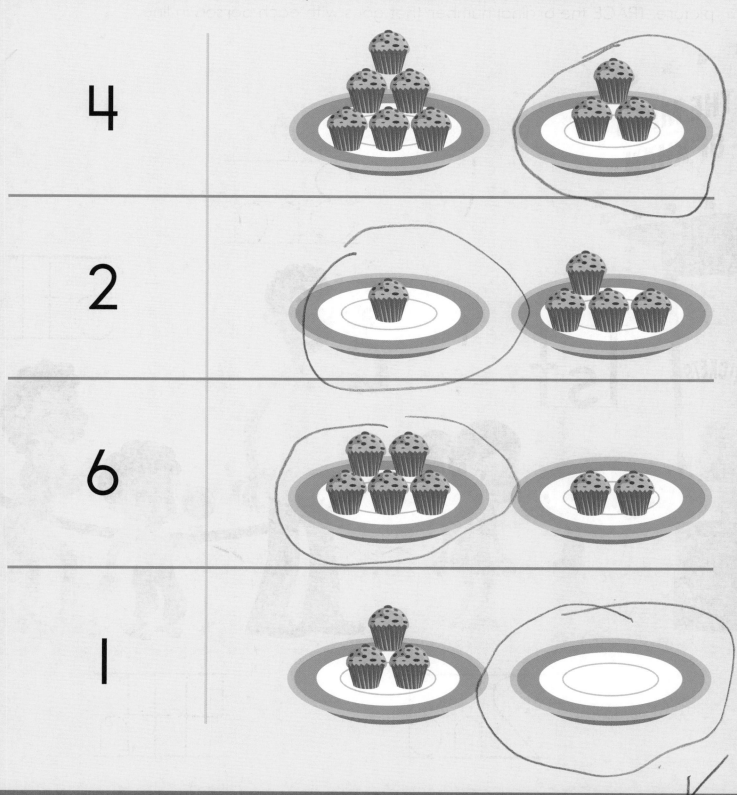

Ordinal Numbers

Practice the Numbers

An **ordinal number** shows order or position, as in "*first* place." FIND each person in the picture. TRACE the ordinal number that goes with each person in line.

7th

9th

6th   8th   10th

Color Groups

COLOR each scoop of ice cream according to the directions.

1st

2nd

3rd

4th

5th

6th

7th

8th

9th

10th

On the Shelf

CIRCLE the book cover for each position on the shelf.

1st

4th

2nd

6th

Beetlemania

LOOK at each number. CIRCLE the correct number of beetles to match that number.

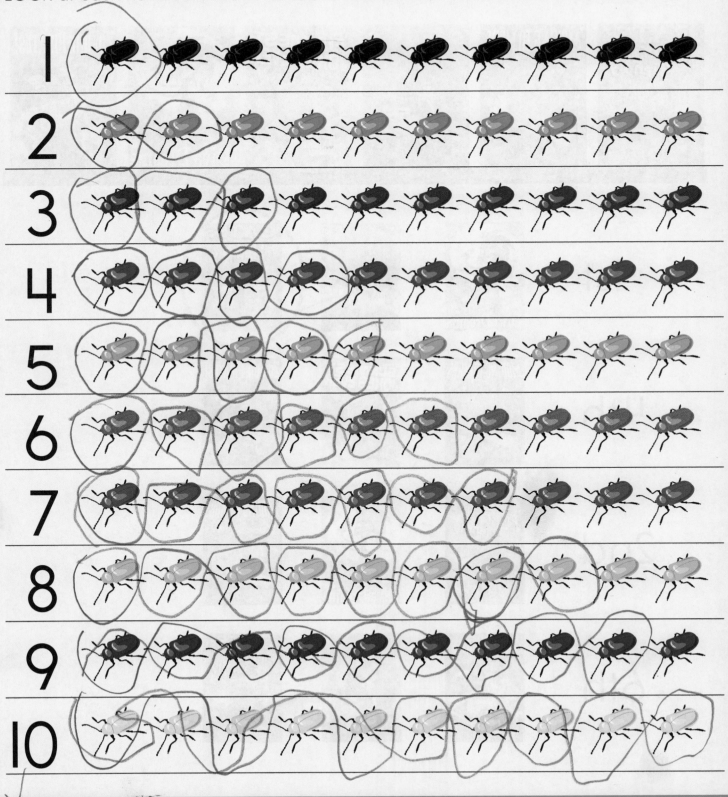

Write the Number

COUNT each group. Then WRITE the number.

5

3

7

2

1

8

4

10

9

6

Load the Truck

DRAW a line to connect each truck with the right loading dock.

Beetlemania

DRAW lines to connect the beetles with the same number of spots.

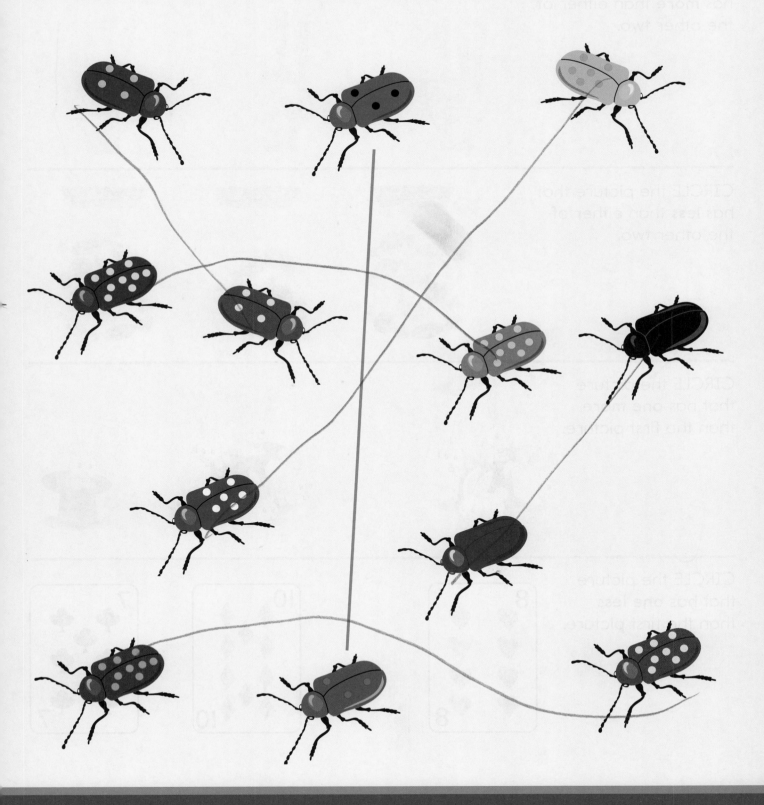

Circle the Picture

CIRCLE the picture that has **more** than either of the other two.

CIRCLE the picture that has **less** than either of the other two.

 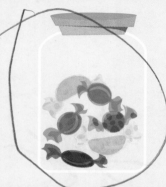 

CIRCLE the picture that has **one more** than the first picture.

CIRCLE the picture that has **one less** than the first picture.

  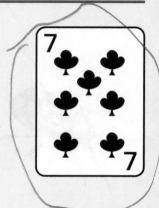

Last Place

COUNT the runners. Then WRITE the ordinal number for the place of the last runner.

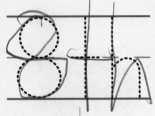

1

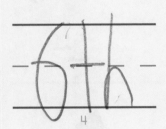

2

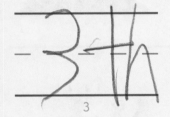

3

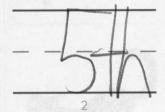

4

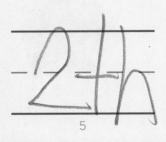

5

Same & Different

Circle the Same

CIRCLE the object in each row that is exactly the same as the first one.

6

Card Tricks

CROSS OUT the pairs of cards that don't match.

Same & Different

Spot the Differences

LOOK at the two pictures. CIRCLE the differences in the second picture.

HINT: There are seven differences.

Same & Different

Odd One Out

CROSS OUT the picture in each row that does **not** go with the others.

Match Up

DRAW lines to connect the socks that go together.

Picture Patterns

Color the Pattern

COLOR the white boxes to finish each pattern.

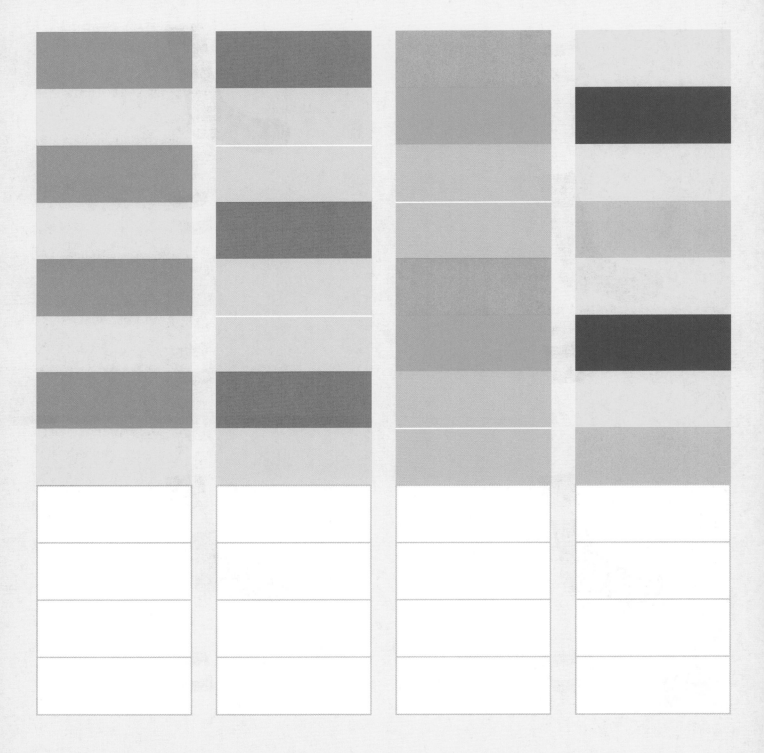

Paint the Fence

COLOR the fence posts to finish each pattern.

Picture Patterns

Draw the Pattern

DRAW the shape that comes next in each pattern.

1.

2.

3.

4.

5.

What Comes Next?

CIRCLE the picture that comes next in each pattern.

1.

2.

3.

4.

Picture Patterns

Draw the Pattern

DRAW the face that comes next in each pattern.

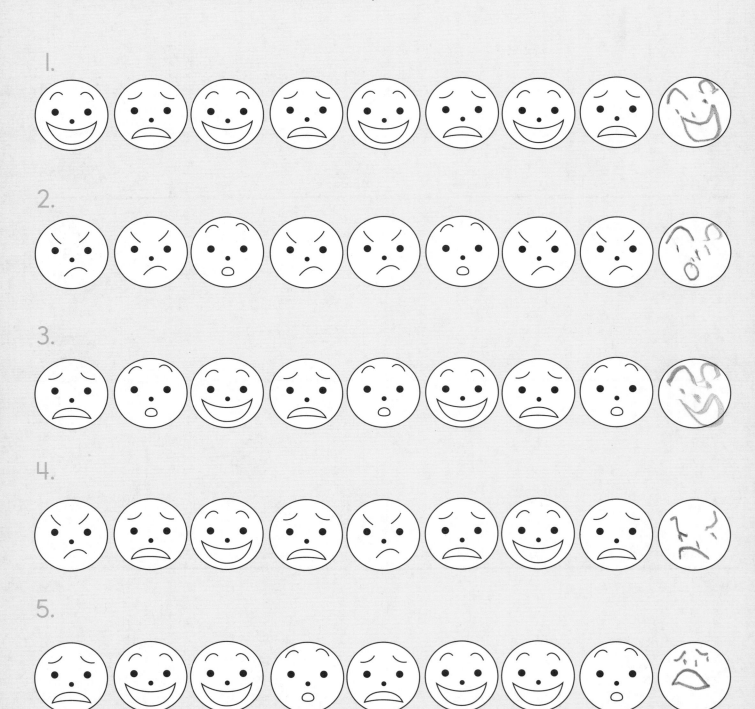

1.

2.

3.

4.

5.

Color the Pattern

COLOR the shapes to finish each pattern.

Number Patterns

Missing Numbers

WRITE the missing number to complete each pattern.

1	2	3	4	5	6

4	5	6	7	8	9

2	3	4	5	6	7

5	6	7	8	9	10

3	4	5	6	7	8

Magic Tricks

CIRCLE the picture that completes each pattern.

Number Patterns

What Comes Next?

CIRCLE the picture that comes next in each pattern.

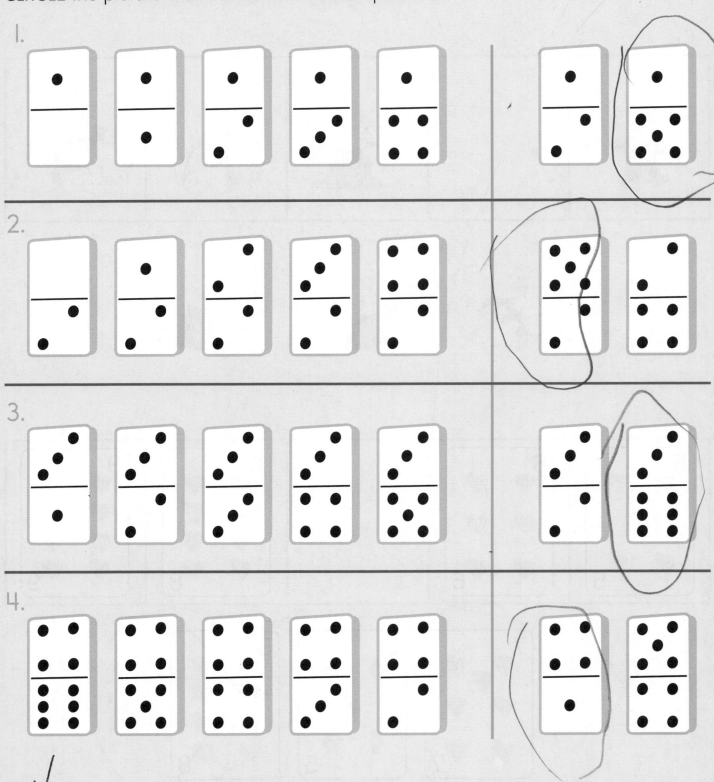

Missing Buttons

WRITE the missing numbers next to the elevator buttons.

Number Patterns

Missing Buttons

WRITE the missing numbers on the buttons.

Missing Numbers

WRITE the missing numbers to complete each pattern.

1	1	10	10
2	2	9	9
3	3	8	8
4	4	7	7
5	5	6	6
6	6	5	5
7	7	4	4
8	8	3	3
9	9	2	2
10	10	1	1

Circle the Same

CIRCLE all of the pictures that are like the top picture.

Odd One Out

CROSS OUT the picture in each row that does **not** go with the others.

Match Up

DRAW lines to connect the numbers and pictures that go together.

8

6

3

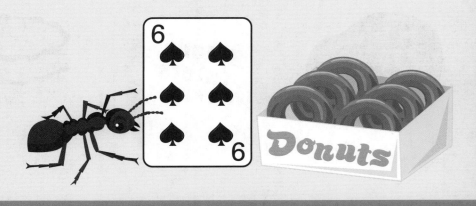

Color Groups

COLOR each picture so that it matches the category.

Match Up

DRAW lines to connect the words and pictures that go together.

Pets

Farm
Animals

Wild
Animals

Odd One Out

CROSS OUT the picture in each row that does **not** go with the others.

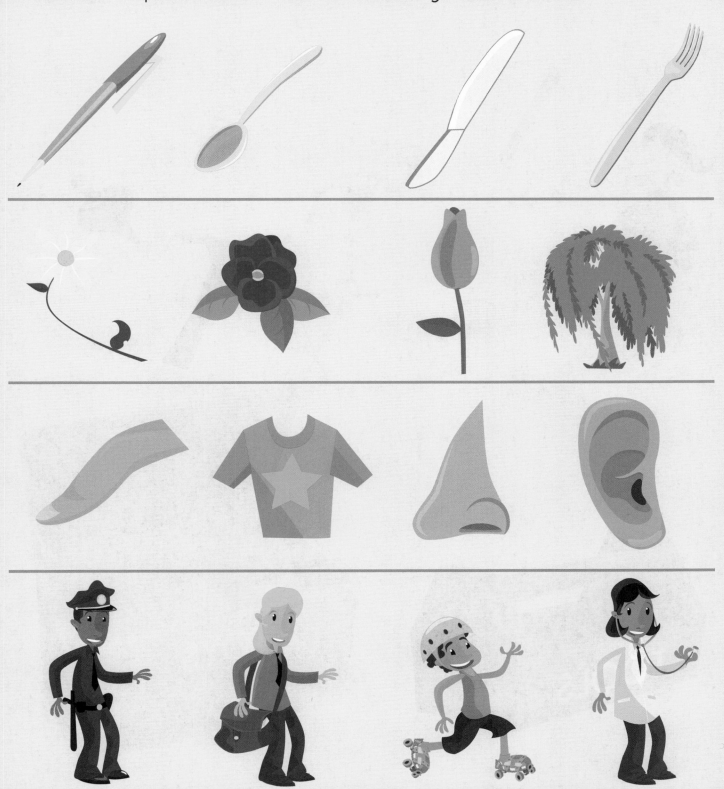

Put It Away

DRAW a line to put each thing in the toy box or the toolbox.

Stack Up

LOOK at the pictures. DRAW a line from each food to the shelf where it belongs.

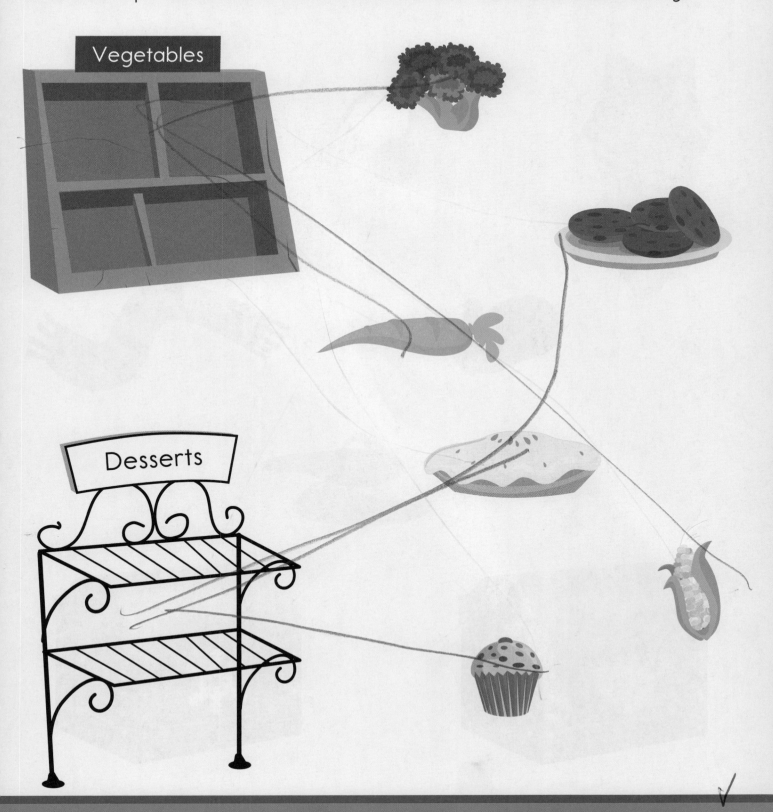

Put It Away

DRAW a line to put each thing in the summer clothes trunk or the winter clothes trunk.

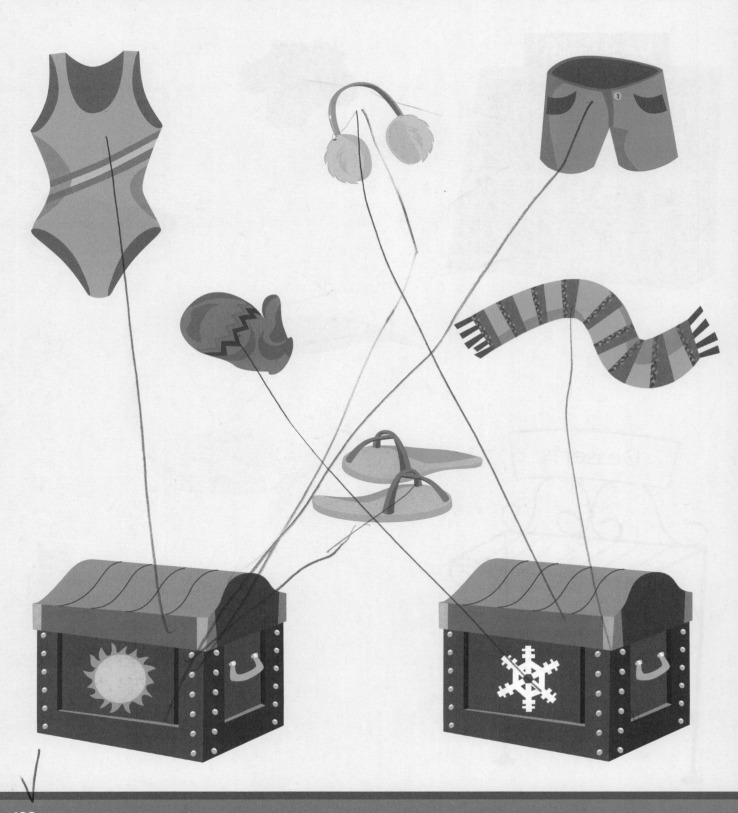

Stack Up

LOOK at the pictures. DRAW a line from each thing to the place where it belongs.

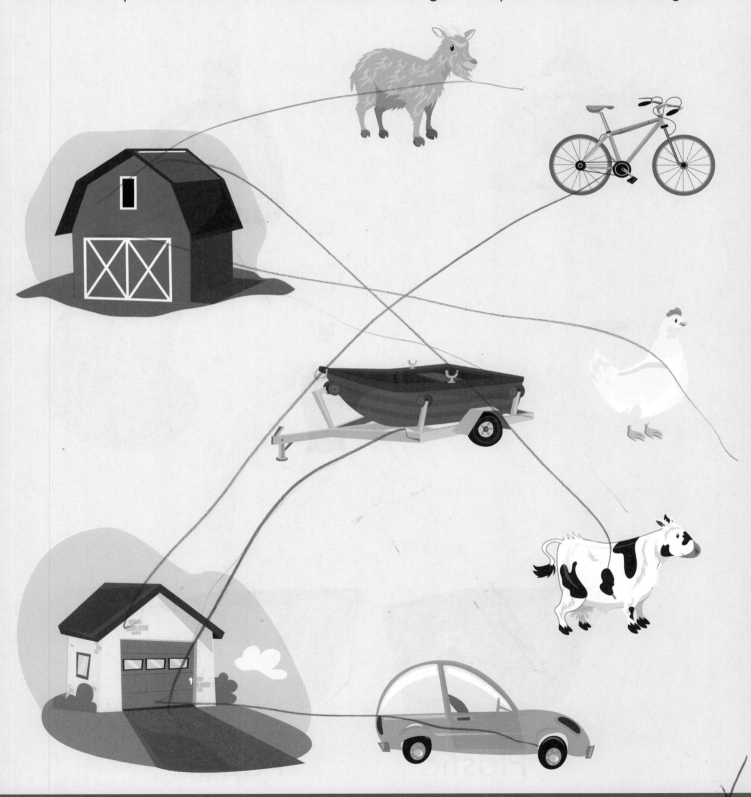

Put It Away

DRAW a line to recycle each object in the plastic or paper bin.

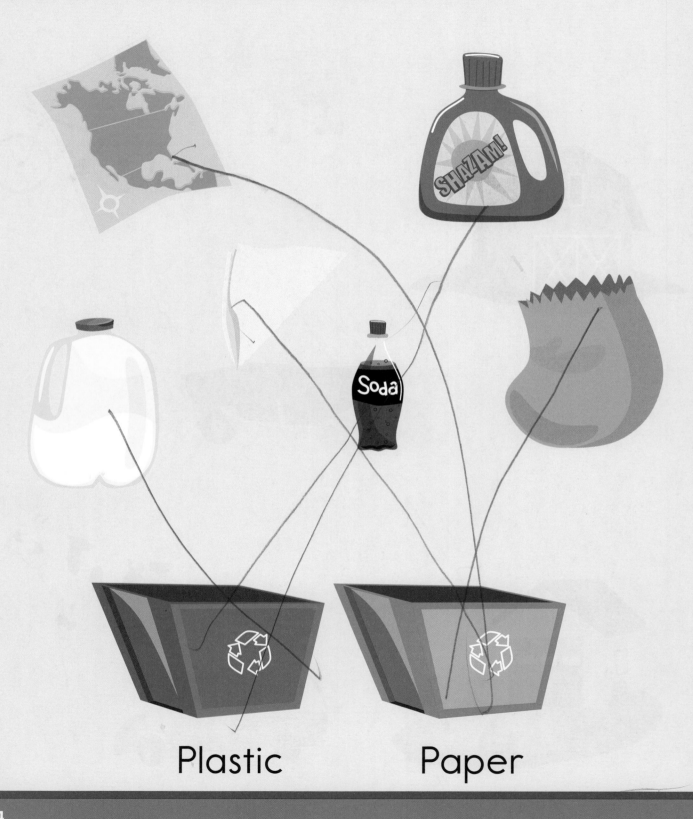

Plastic

Paper

Get in Place

DRAW a line from each picture outside the diagram to show where it belongs inside the diagram.

Beetlemania

CIRCLE the beetle that does **not** belong in each group.

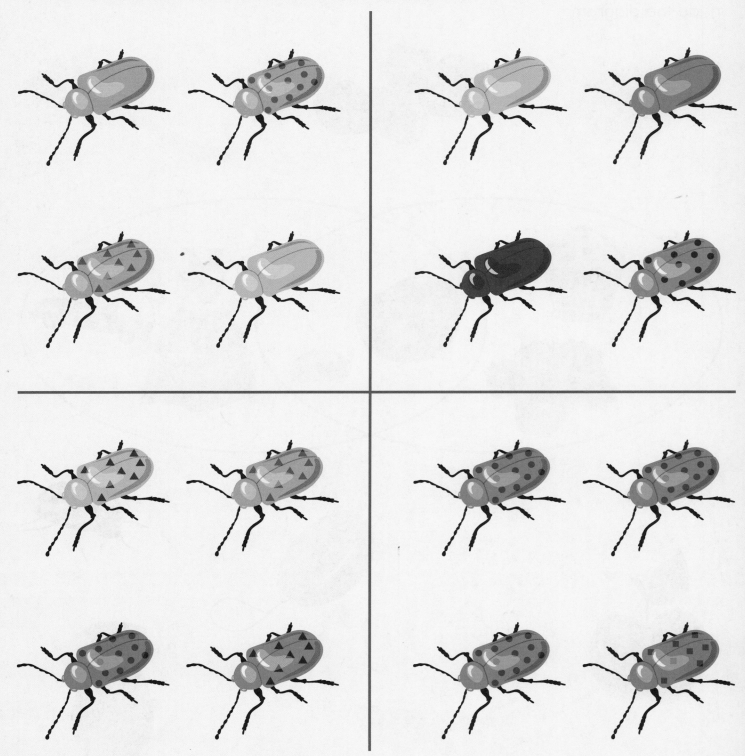

Finish the Pattern

WRITE the numbers or letters to complete each pattern.

| 1 | 2 | 3 | 4 | 5 | 6 | 7 | 8 |

| 2 | 3 | 4 | 5 | 6 | 7 | 8 | 9 |

| 3 | 4 | 5 | 6 | 7 | 8 | 9 | 10 |

| X | O | O | X | O | O | X | O | O | X | O | O |

| X | O | O | X | X | O | O | X | X | O | O | X |

| X | X | O | X | X | O | X | X | O | X | X | O |

Beetlemania

CIRCLE the beetle that comes next in each pattern.

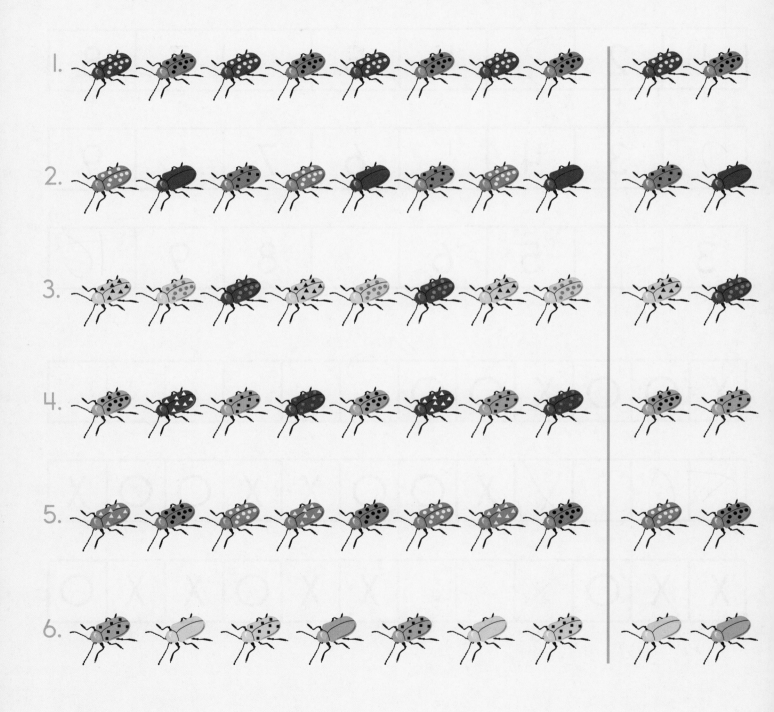

Load the Truck

DRAW a line to connect each truck with the right loading dock.

Spot the Differences

LOOK at the two pictures. CIRCLE the differences in the second picture.

HINT: There are three differences.

Color the Pattern

COLOR the shapes to finish each pattern.

Odd One Out

CIRCLE the picture in each row that does **not** go with the others.

Now WRITE what all of the circled pictures have in common.

They are all insects.
They are fly, ant and ladybug.

Recognizing Shapes

Color the Circles

COLOR all of the circles.

Color the Triangles

COLOR all of the triangles.

Recognizing Shapes

Color the Rectangles

COLOR all of the rectangles.

HINT: A square is a special kind of rectangle.

Bubble Pop

LOOK at the bubbles. CROSS OUT the bubbles that are **not** circles.

Circle the Same

CIRCLE all of the triangles.

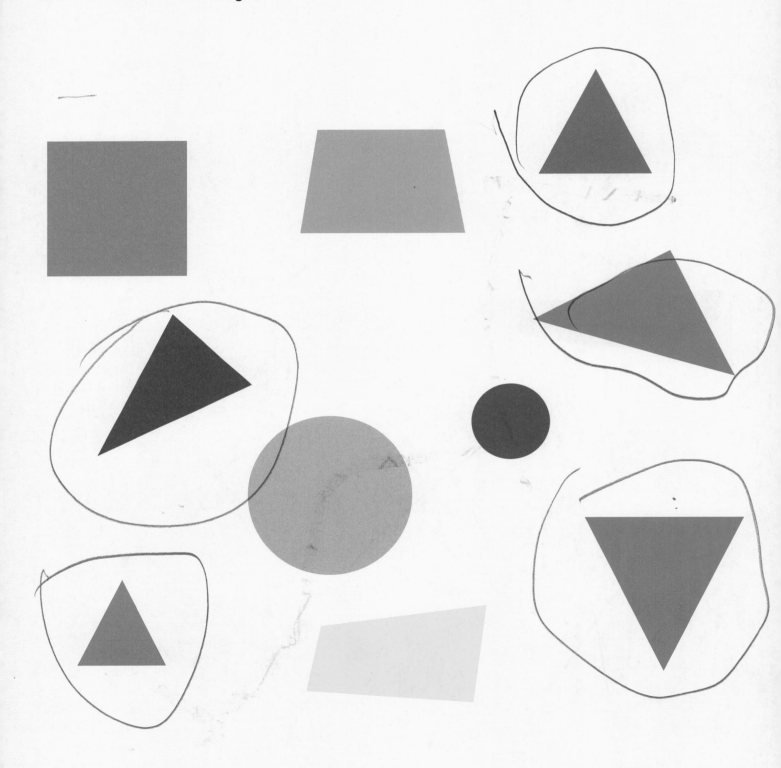

Pond Crossing

DRAW a line following the rectangles to help the frog jump across the pond.

HINT: A square is a special kind of rectangle.

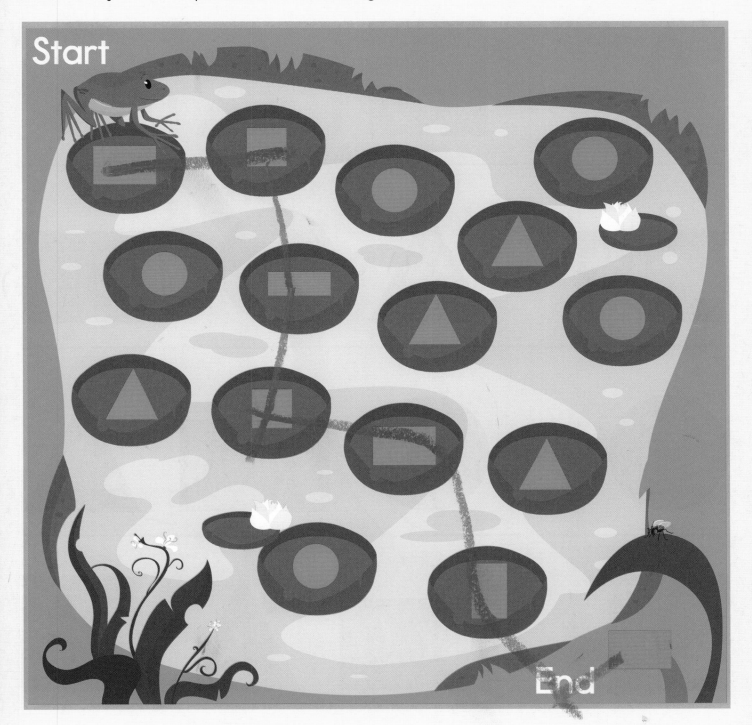

Recognizing Shapes

Circle the Same

CIRCLE the shape in each row that is the same shape as the first one.

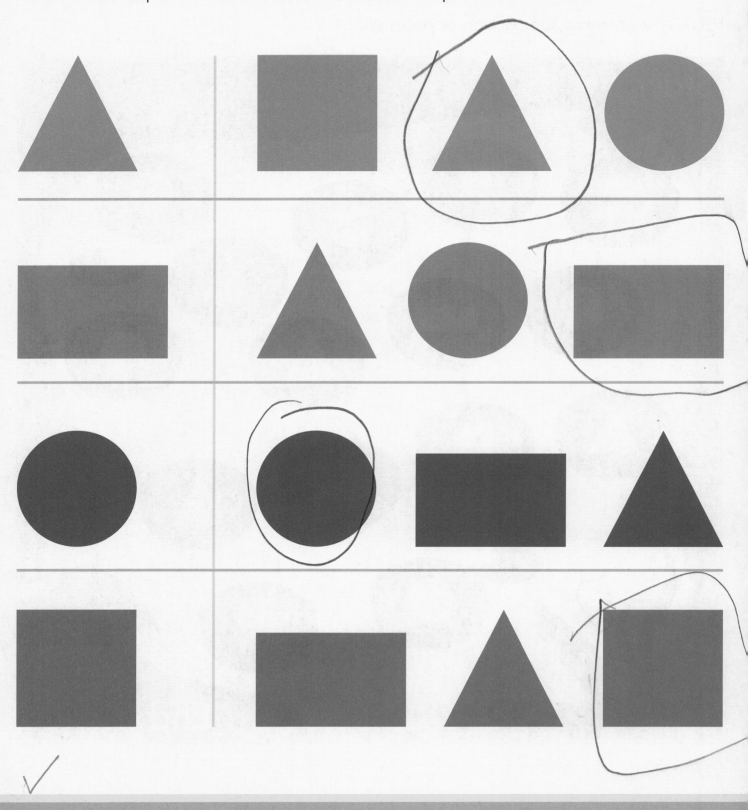

Hide and Seek

How many of each shape can you find in the picture? WRITE the number next to each shape.

 5    3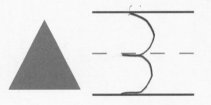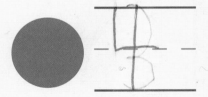

Drawing & Comparing Shapes

Trace and Draw

TRACE each shape. Then DRAW more of the same shape.

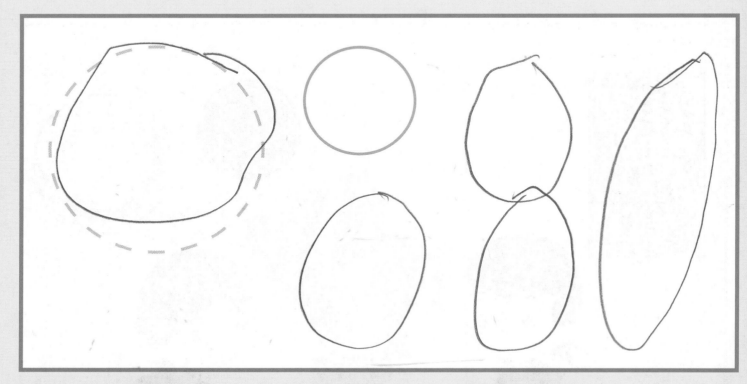

Small, Smaller, Smallest

CIRCLE the **smaller** shape.

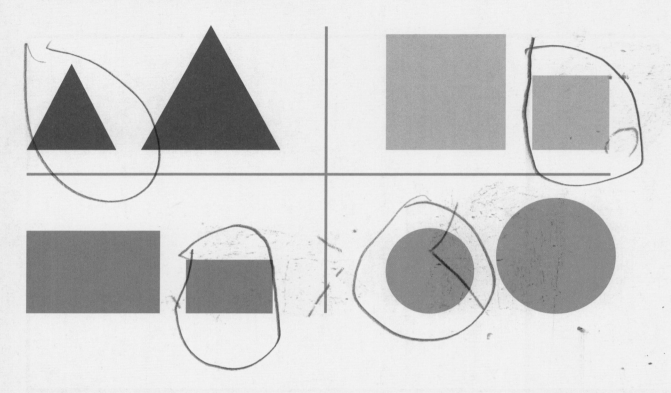

CIRCLE the **smallest** shape.

Big, Bigger, Biggest

COLOR the **bigger** shape.

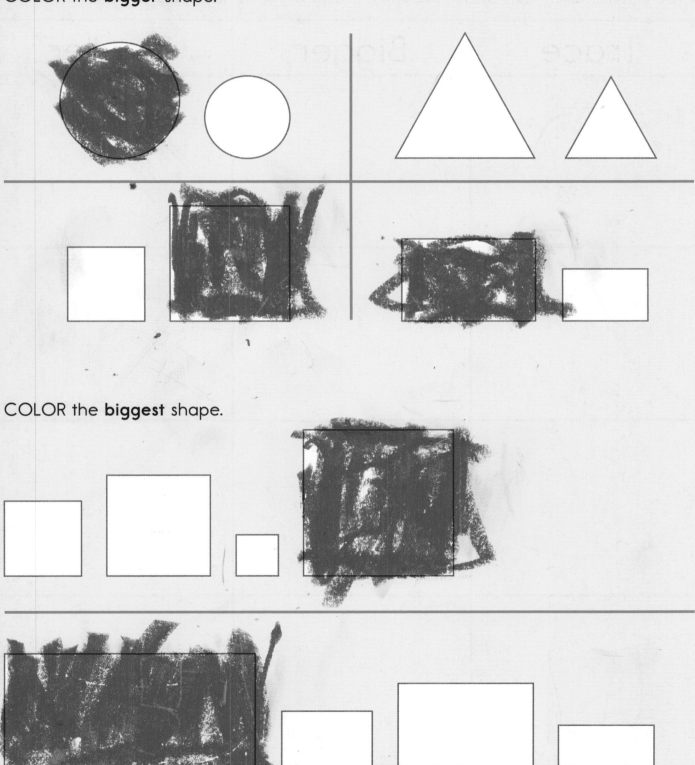

COLOR the **biggest** shape.

Drawing & Comparing Shapes

Trace and Draw

TRACE each shape. Then DRAW the same shape bigger and smaller.

Trace	Bigger	Smaller

Circle the Same

CIRCLE the shape in each row that is exactly the same as the first one.

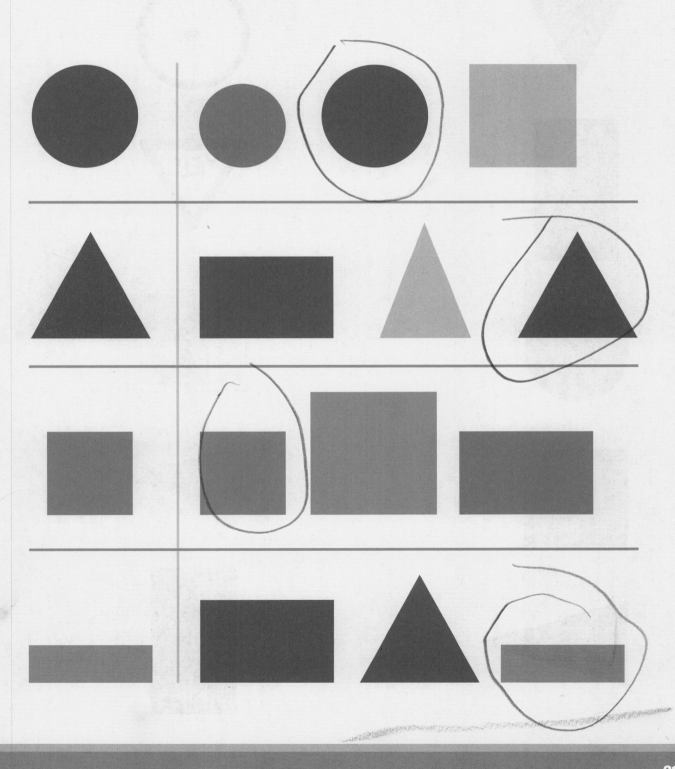

Drawing & Comparing Shapes

Match Up

DRAW lines to connect the shapes that are the same.

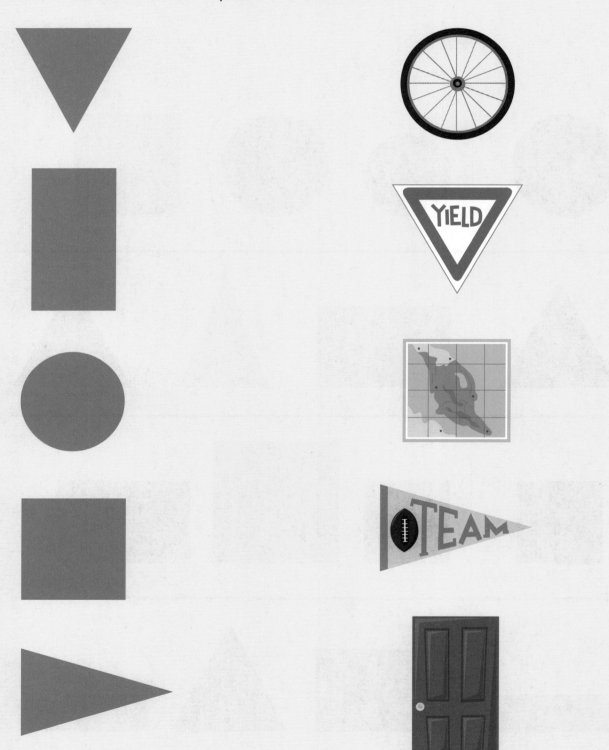

Odd One Out

CROSS OUT the picture in each row that does **not** go with the others.

   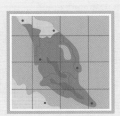

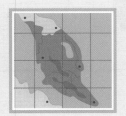   

Which One?

TRACE the triangle that is **over** another shape.

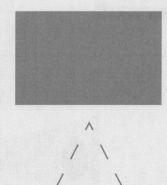

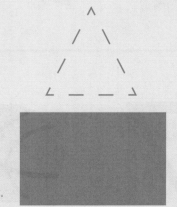

At the Market

FIND each food in the picture, and CIRCLE the food that is **under** it in the market.

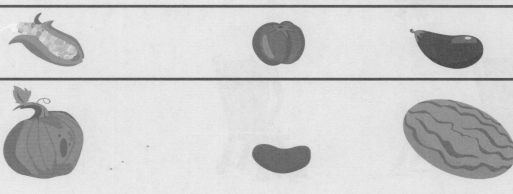

1.

2.

3.

4.

I Smell a Rat

FIND the rat in each picture, and CIRCLE the picture in each pair where the rat is **below** an object.

On the Shelf

FIND each book in the picture, and CIRCLE the book that is **above** it on the shelf.

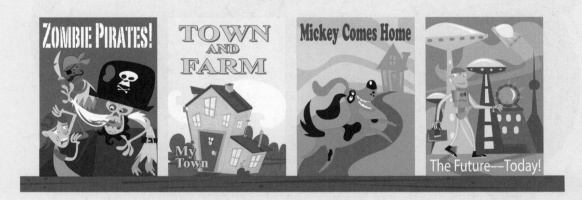

1.

2.

3.

4.

Beetlemania

DRAW a line connecting each beetle with its matching hole.

HINT: Look at the shape on each beetle's back.

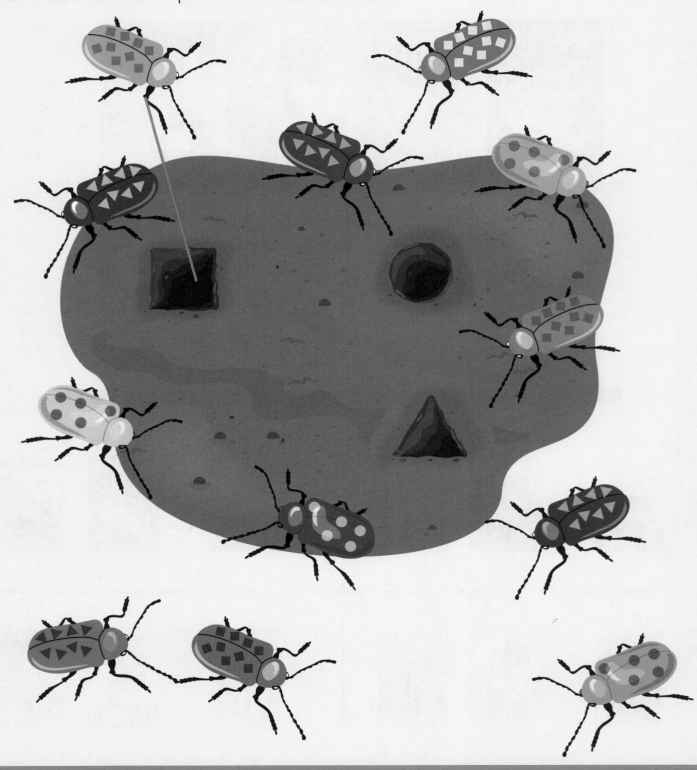

Circle It

CIRCLE the shape that matches each group of shapes.

1.

2.

3.

4.

Load the Truck

DRAW a line to connect each truck with the right loading dock.

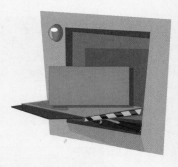

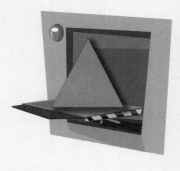

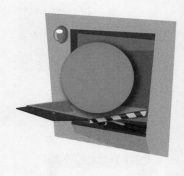

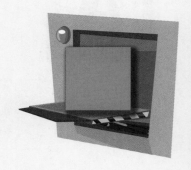

Shape Shifter

DRAW a circle below the ■ .

DRAW a triangle above the ● .

DRAW a square over the ▲ .

DRAW a rectangle under the ● .

Length

Which One?

CIRCLE the picture in each pair that is **longer** than the other.

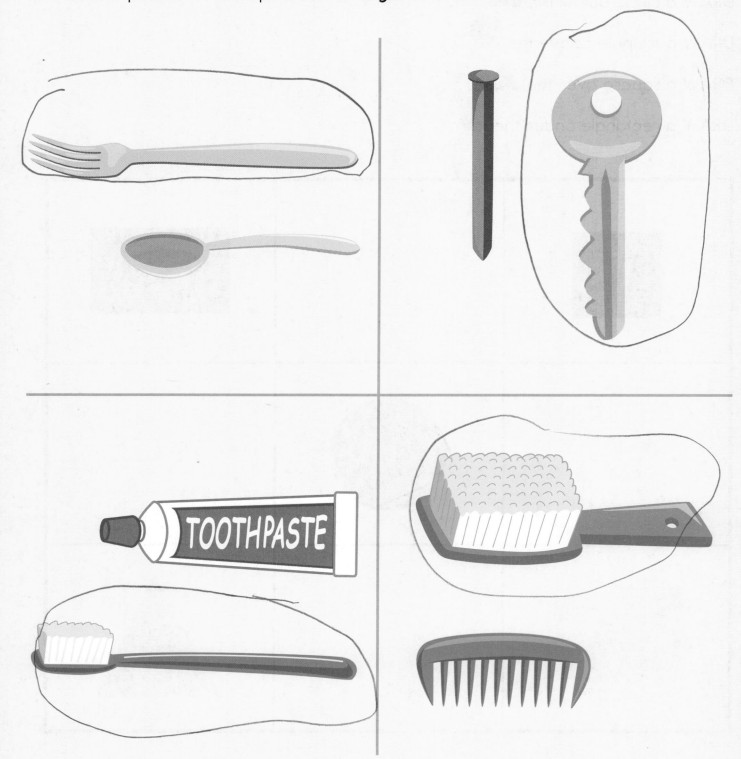

Which One?

CIRCLE the picture in each pair that is **shorter** than the other.

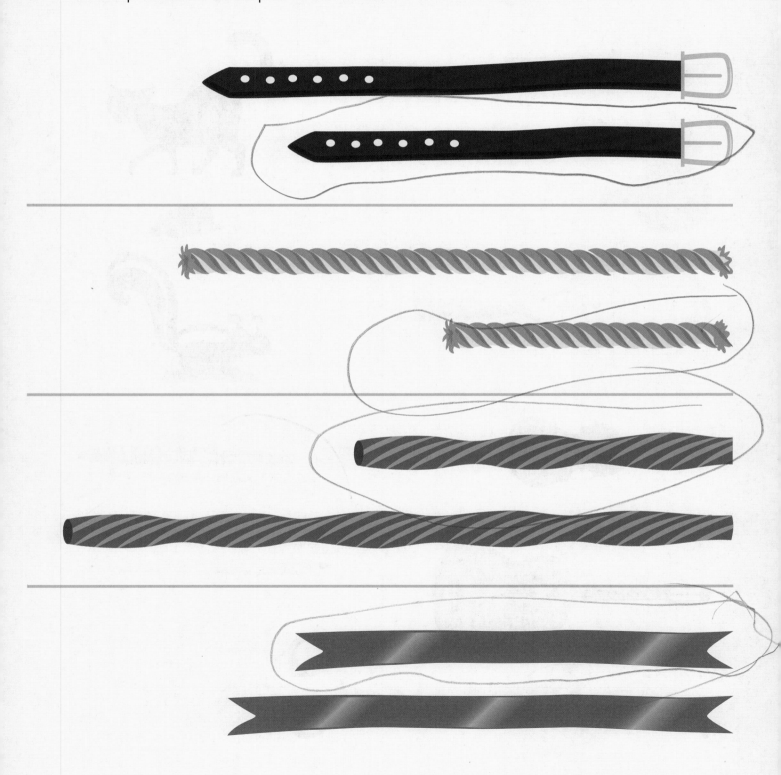

Length

Circle the Same

CIRCLE the picture in each section that is about the same length as the top picture.

Where Will It Fit?

DRAW a line between each beam and the place where it will fit on the building.

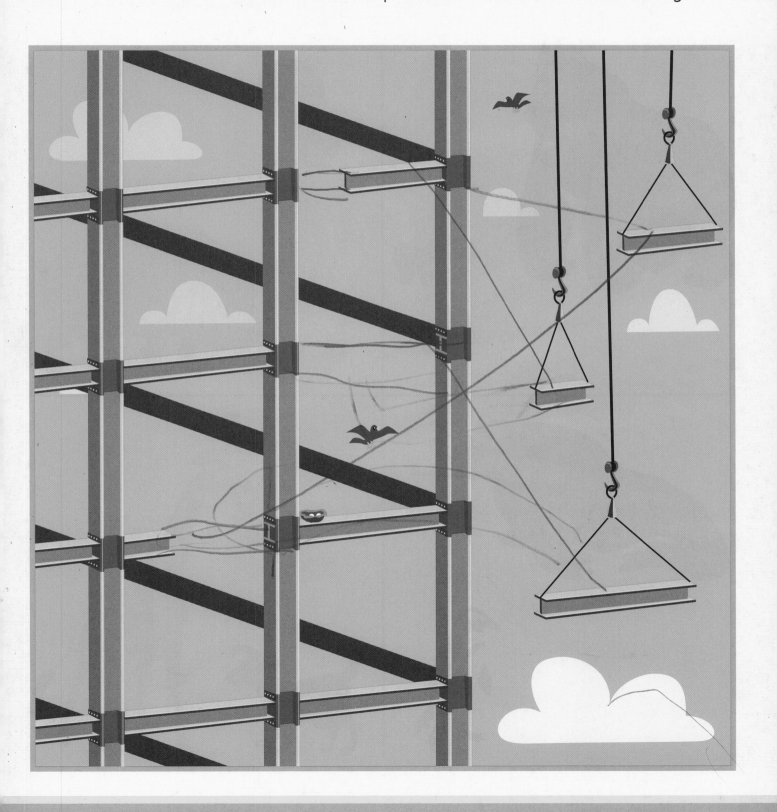

Weight

Which One?

CIRCLE the picture of the object in each pair that is **heavier** than the other.

Which One?

CIRCLE the picture in each pair that is **lighter** than the other.

Match Up

DRAW lines to connect the objects that weigh about the same.

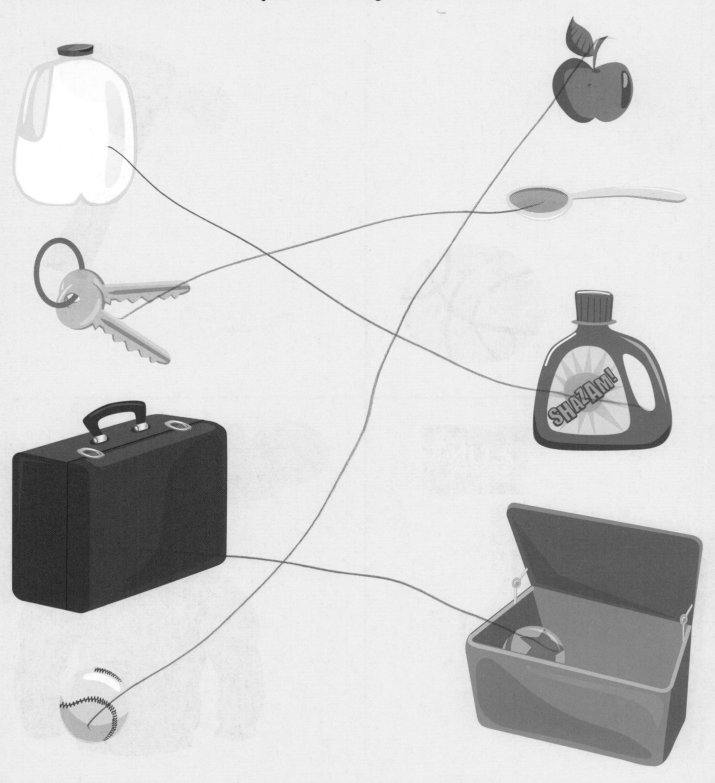

Can He Lift It?

The heaviest thing Jimmy can lift is a car.
CIRCLE all of the things that Jimmy can lift.

Thirst Quencher

CIRCLE the picture of the thing in each pair that holds **more** than the other.

At the Beach

CIRCLE the picture of the thing in each pair that holds **less** than the other.

Volume

Match Up

DRAW a line between each object and the box it best fits inside.

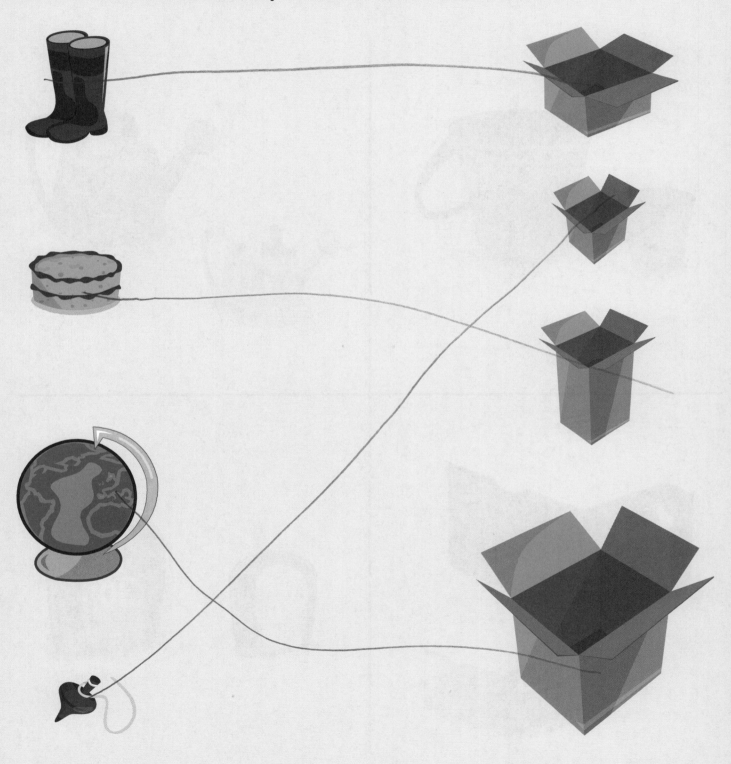

Lemonade Stand

CIRCLE the object in each pair that can hold **more** than the other.

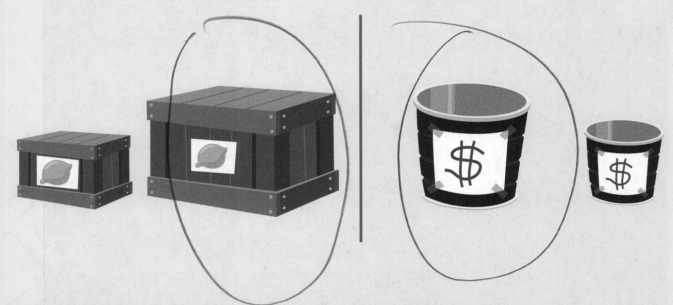

CIRCLE the object in each pair that can hold **less** than the other.

Beetlemania

TRACE the longer line in each pair of bug trails.

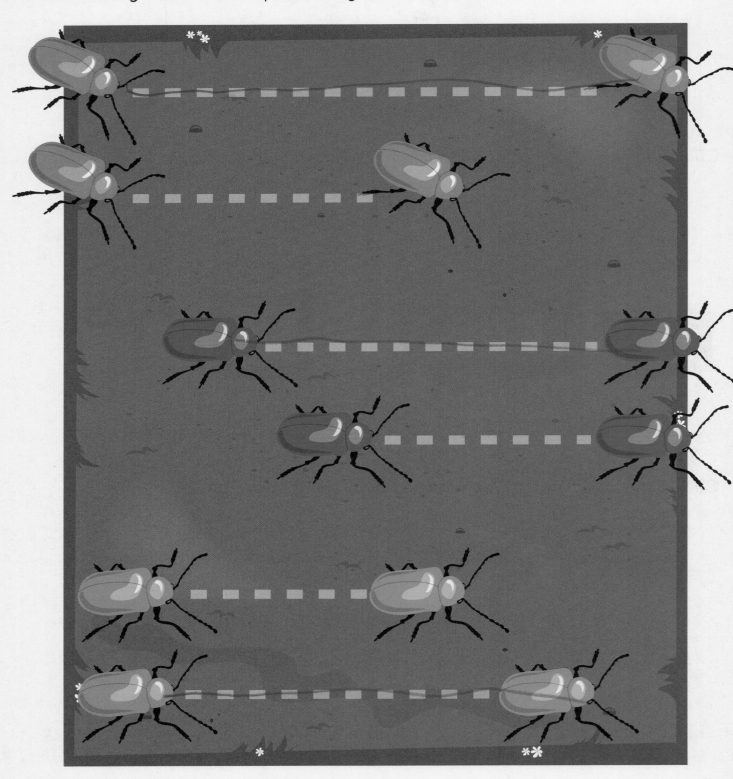

Match the Picture

DRAW a line to connect the elephant to each **heavy** object and the feather to each **light** object.

Heavy	Light

Review

Unit Rewind

DRAW a line that is longer than the red line and shorter than the green line.

_____

_____

COLOR the object in each pair that is lighter than the other.

Unit Rewind

CIRCLE the object in each pair that holds more than the other.

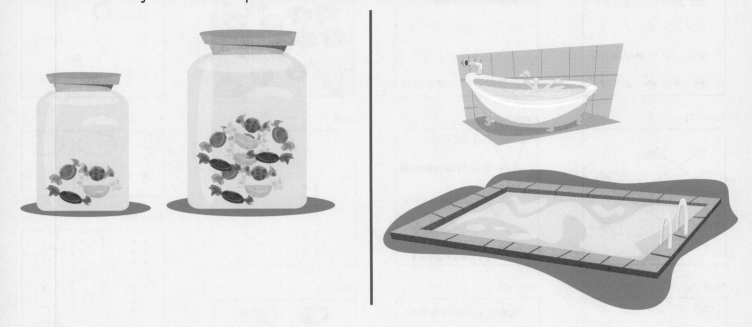

COLOR the object in each pair that holds less than the other.

Answers

Page 131
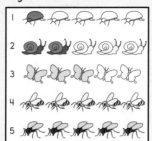

Page 141
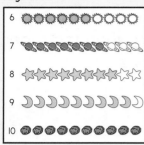

Page 146
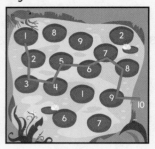

Page 152

Page 132
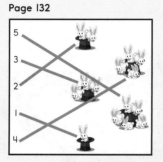

Page 142
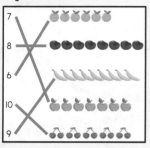

Page 147
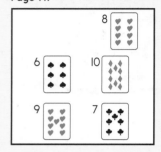

Page 153

Page 154
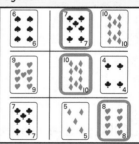

Page 133
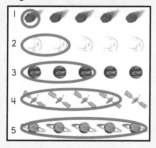

Page 143
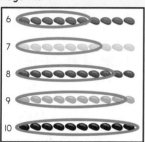

Page 149
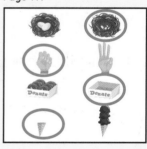

Page 155
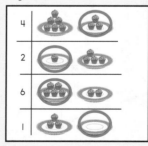

Page 134
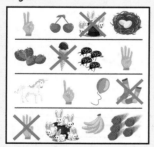

Page 144

Page 150
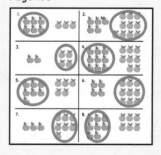

Page 158

Page 135

Page 145

Page 151
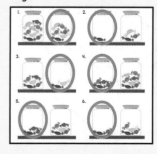

Answers

Page 159

1st
4th
2nd
6th

Page 160

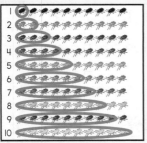

Page 161

	5	3
	7	2
	1	8
	4	10
	9	6

Page 162

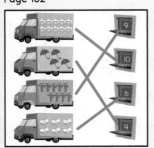

Page 163

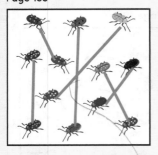

Page 164

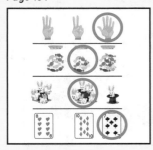

Page 165

1. 8th
2. 5th
3. 3rd
4. 6th
5. 2nd

Page 166

Page 167

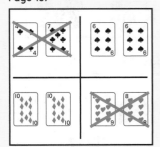

Pages 168-69

Page 170

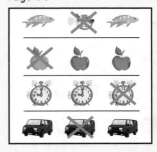

Page 171

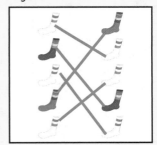

Page 172

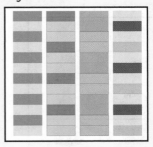

Page 173

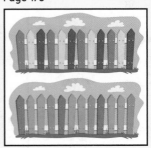

Page 174

1.
2.
3.
4.
5.

Page 175

1.
2.
3.
4.

Page 176

1.
2.
3.
4.
5.

Page 177

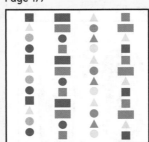

Page 178

1	2	3	4	5	6
4	5	6	7	8	9
2	3	4	5	6	7
5	6	7	8	9	10
3	4	5	6	7	8

Page 179

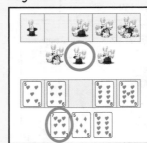

Answers

Page 180

1.
2.
3.
4.

Page 181

Page 182

Page 183

1	1	10	10
2	2	9	9
3	3	8	8
4	4	7	7
5	5	6	6
6	6	5	5
7	7	4	4
8	8	3	3
9	9	2	2
10	10	1	1

Page 184

Page 185

Page 186

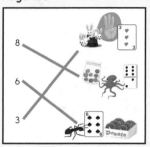

Page 187
Suggestions:

Page 188

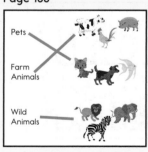

Page 189

Page 190

Page 191

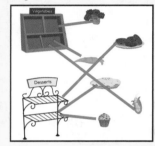

Page 192

Page 193

Page 194

Page 195

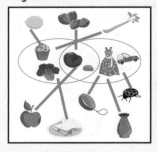

Page 196

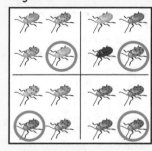

Page 197

1	2	3	4	5	6	7	8
2	3	4	5	6	7	8	9
3	4	5	6	7	8	9	10

X	O	O	X	O	O	X	O	O	X	O	O
X	O	O	X	X	O	O	X	X	O	O	X
X	X	O	X	O	X	X	O	X	X	O	O

Page 198

1.
2.
3.
4.
5.
6.

Page 199

Answers

Page 200

Page 201

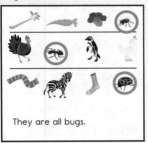

They are all bugs.

Page 202

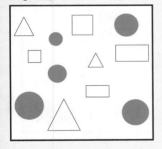

Page 203

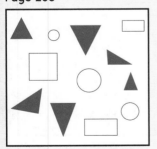

Page 204

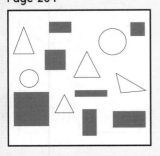

Page 205

Page 206

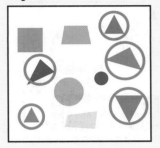

Page 207

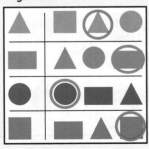

Page 208

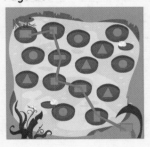

Page 209

Remember, a square is a special kind of rectangle.

Note: The eyes are ovals, not circles.

Page 212

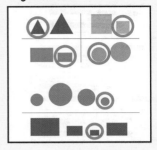

Page 213

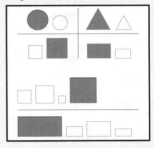

Page 214

Suggestions:

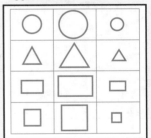

Page 215

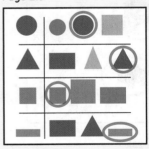

Page 216

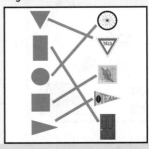

Pages 217

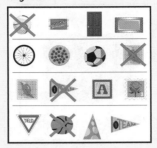

Page 218

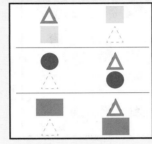

Page 219

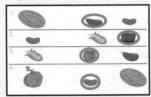

Page 220

Page 221

Answers

Page 222
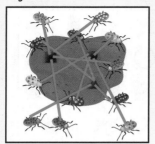

Page 227
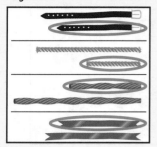

Page 232

Page 237

Page 223
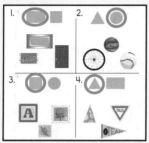

Page 228

Page 233

Page 238

Page 224
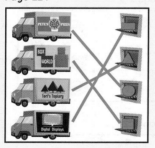

Page 229
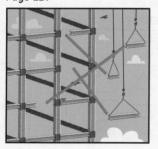

Page 234

Page 239
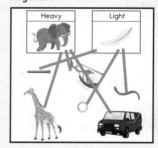

Page 225
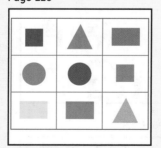

Page 230

Page 235

Page 240

Page 226
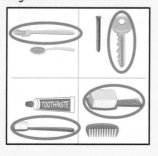

Page 231

Page 236
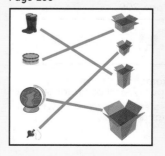

Page 241

Sylvan for Every Student!

SINGLE-SUBJECT WORKBOOKS

☑ Focus on individual skills and subjects

☑ Fun activities and grade-appropriate exercises

3-IN-1 SUPER WORKBOOKS

☑ Three Sylvan single-subject workbooks in one package for just $18.99!

☑ Perfect practice for the student who needs to focus on a range of topics

FUN ON THE RUN ACTIVITY BOOKS

☑ Just $3.99/$4.75 Can.

☑ Colorful games and activities for on-the-go learning

FLASHCARD SETS

☑ Spelling and vocabulary for Pre-K–5th grade

☑ Math for Pre-K–5th grade

PAGE PER DAY WORKBOOKS

☑ Perforated pages—perfect for your child to do just one workbook page each day

☑ Extra practice the easy way!

KICK START PACKAGES

☑ Includes books, flashcards, access to online activities, and more

☑ Everything your child needs in one comprehensive package

Try FREE pages today at SylvanPagePerDay.com

Sylvan Learning

SPECIAL OFFER FROM

Congratulations on your Sylvan product purchase! Your child is now on the way to building skills for academic success. Sylvan would like to extend a special offer for a discount on our exclusive Sylvan Skills Assessment® to you and your family. Bring this coupon to your scheduled assessment to receive your discount. Limited time offer.* One per family.

You are entitled to a $10 DISCOUNT on a Sylvan Skills Assessment®.

It includes a comprehensive evaluation of your child's needs using our unique combination of standardized tests, teacher observations, and personal interviews. This assessment is the key to creating a personal learning plan just for your child, targeting those exact skills your child needs.

Visit SylvanLearningProducts.com/coupon today to find a participating location and schedule your Sylvan Skills Assessment®.

* Offer expires December 31, 2014. Valid at participating locations.
Offer will be valued at local currency equivalent on date of registration with Sylvan Learning.

CUT ALONG THE DOTTED LINE

Moms, Dads, Teachers, and Homeschoolers Give Rave Reviews!

"**Samantha loves these books** because to her, they are not schoolwork. They are fun activities. But really she is learning, and doing the same work she does at school."
—MommyMandy.com

"As an early childhood teacher, I know that good reading, vocabulary, and spelling skills make an essential foundation for both academic success as well as lifelong learning. **Sylvan Learning Workbooks & Learning Kits** are an awesome resource that I'd have no problem recommending to the parents of any of my students who are struggling."
—TheOpinionatedParent.com

"As a teacher, I look for different aspects in a resource than a student or a parent might. . . . **The book has vibrant, attractive colors, and the worksheets are really fun.** My 10-year-old son has been enjoying them since I got the book. . . . I recommend this book to students, parents, and teachers alike for increasing student achievement."
—DynamiteLessonPlan.com

"If you are looking for some **good, fun learning books for your child**, I definitely recommend the Sylvan Learning series."
—TheDadJam.com

1000